ABOUT EMMA

In the tale of *Rumpelstiltskin*, the miller's daughter has to weave straw into gold because of her father's overly enthusiastic claims. In a modern-day fairytale, Emma Zimmerman has taken her dad's obsession for heritage grains and transformed it into an award-winning flour business. Her alchemy also finds expression in the home kitchen, where she turns these unusual flours and grains into accessible and tasty meals, much to the delight of her friends and family. Emma's passion for historical restoration extends beyond grains; with her husband, she restored a burned out one-hundred-year-old house in downtown Phoenix, where they now live with their three sweet children and an affectionate pit bull. Emma tends an amateur garden and is just waiting for someone to ask her about the status of her compost pile.

UNUSUAL FLOURS & HERITAGE GRAINS
STORIES AND RECIPES FROM HAYDEN FLOUR MILLS

The Miller's Daughter

EMMA ZIMMERMAN

Hardie Grant

BOOKS

INTRO

My dad and I have a rule: he's only allowed to tell me one new idea a day. My dad hemorrhages ideas. He still works his day job and I run the day-to-day operations of the mill, so he usually calls me at nine o'clock every morning from his cubicle, eager to meet his daily idea quota. How I dread that call. By my count, one great idea for 'improving' the business means hundreds of hours of work for me. But curiosity always gets the better of me, and I pick up the phone.

Over the last three years, I've developed a few strategies for defusing his idea-bombs besides simply rolling my eyes and saying, 'That is the worst idea I've ever heard'. That gets old and makes me feel like I'm still his teenage daughter and not his business partner. For a while, I tried what I call 'escalation' – taking his crazy ideas and making them even more extreme. He'll say, 'I have some ideas for our new labels! How about a puppy or a baby eating polenta?' and I'll say, 'Great idea Dad, but you know what would be even better? A baby eating polenta while riding on top of a puppy!' The idea gets so absurd that it quietly withers and blows away in the wind. But this tactic has also been known to backfire on me. When my over-the-top idea actually sticks, I've inadvertently landed myself in an acre of wheat with nothing but an old-fashioned scythe in hand to harvest it.

Another tactic I try is called 'preemptive ideation'. I pick up the phone, and before he can say hello, I blurt out, 'I have the best idea. You know how we have all those leftover middlings from the mill? Why don't we get a few pigs, feed them the middlings and sell bacon just like Charles Hayden did in 1874?' The role swap momentarily confuses him and takes the wind right out of his little idea-boat sails. And I've pretty much insured myself against ever having to raise pigs on top of everything else I do.

But I do have to remind myself that I owe my dream job to one of my dad's harebrained ideas. In 2009, I was working on a PhD at McGill University when he called to tell me about his idea to restart the historic Hayden Flour Mills in my hometown of Tempe, Arizona. The genius part

It really does matter what grains we grow, how we grow them and how we mill them.

about it, the part that hooked me, was that he didn't want to bother with restoring the iconic silos; he wanted to restart the original Hayden Flour Mills in the spirit of its founder, Charles Hayden. From its beginning in 1864, the mill used the power of the Salt River to stone mill a variety of wheat brought over by European missionaries in the 1600s.

My dad grew up on a diversified farm in North Dakota and saw the industrialization of wheat farming unfold in his lifetime. My great-grandfather harvested his grain with a scythe and field thresher, my grandfather had a little John Deere ride-on combine, and today my dad's cousin has a GPS-controlled combine that could swallow my grandpa's John Deere whole. Dad saw the wheat on his family farm get shorter and shorter with the advent of get-rich-quick modern seed varieties. These modern varieties were engineered for the convenience of roller milling and became the substrates of Wonder Bread and the like.

For us, opening a stone mill and growing old grains was a great big experiment to see if any of that really mattered. To discover if the industrialization of milling and farming was to blame for the boring, flavorless bread we are all so used to. Almost a decade in, our answer is unequivocally yes. It really does matter what grains we grow, how we grow them and how we mill them. And I hope you'll agree by the time you finish this book.

LEFT

The historic Hayden Flour Mills in Tempe, Arizona, was founded in 1874 and closed in 1998.

THE MILLER'S DAUGHTER

I love it when I travel and people say, 'You can grow wheat in Arizona?' because then I get to say very proudly, 'Actually, we can grow some of the best wheat in the world!' And when I'm feeling especially patriotic, I add: 'Arizona used to be called a bread basket! And our wheat fields fed armies!' But that was a long time ago. Today, most of our grain crops are for feed and the rest are for export, so in a way these skeptics are right.

The land that grew those crops all that time ago is still here and still fertile, and we are making our own small dent in the steady stream of grain going to cattle feed and export crops. In our first year, we grew 30 acres of wheat. Ten years on, we have almost 400 acres of wheat in production.

This book is full of recipes, but the way I've learned to use these grains is woven into our own Western (a spaghetti Western, if you'll allow me ...) – the tall tale of an unlikely underdog rising from the Wild West, on the outskirts of rural Phoenix, where the dreamers are still pioneering new territory in an agriculture overrun by homogenized grain farming. We are growing the forgotten historic grains no one else is bothering to grow; we're tossing dried beans and grape seeds into the mill because there are no rules; we're restoring rusty old mills we scrounge on eBay; and we're losing entire crops at a time because there are no experts when it comes to this brand-new adventure. It isn't all a glamorous success story, but we keep on growing and milling these grains because they spark our curiosity and wonder. And we can't resist these bizarre-looking grains with names like Tibetan Purple Barley, Blue Beard Durum, Blue Tinge Farro, Rouge de Bordeaux and Red Fife.

I knew that if I quit my PhD program and moved home to help my dad restart the Hayden Flour Mills, I'd have a great big pile of memoir-worthy stories. And I do. Over the last few years, I've gotten to meet grouchy farmers, brilliant chefs, wise seed savers, celebrities, kind-hearted millers, and a whole cast of storybook characters.

What follows is the true story of how we restarted Arizona's historic Hayden Flour Mills and rescued obscure grains from the brink of extinction, and what we ate along the way.

SOW

'DID OUR FIRST COMMUNION WITH FELLOW HUMANS
ALSO PLACE US IN WITH GRAPES,
GRAINS, YEASTS, SALT AND WATER,
SO THAT EACH AND EVERY ONE OF US WERE BLESSED
IN THE BAKING AND THE BREAKING OF THE BREAD,
IN FERMENTING AND IMBIBING BLOOD-RED WINE
UNTIL ALL THEIR MOLECULES DANCED IN OURS?'
'First Communion' by Brother Coyote

My dad likes to claim that he arranged my marriage. He ran into my future husband at the grocery store and, recognizing him as a familiar face from my high school track meets, invited him over for dinner. This single invitation slowly morphed into a standing weekly dinner invitation from my parents to any of my or my siblings' friends. And future-husband didn't miss a week. I made a habit of ignoring him and retreated to my room after dinner to study, but he just kept hanging around. For all I knew, he was there for my parents' cooking or my prettier sister.

In those college days, lots of 'guy friends' stopped by my parents' house around dinner time. I don't blame them – old-fashioned family dinners are a dying ritual, and my parents' hospitality is legendary. My mom always built a balanced menu of color, nutrients and spice, and my dad usually added a hackneyed kitchen experiment for an element of theater and delight: a ham cooked in hay, freshly roasted coffee, jars of lacto-fermenting vegetables, a freshly butchered chicken from a farmer friend, dining with only pocket-knives to pretend we were French peasants, homemade sushi … and there was always a loaf of homemade bread. I realized that the simple family dinner I had taken for granted my whole life was not a given for most of our peers, and they craved a seat at that table.

As much as it sometimes annoys me that my husband isn't as passionate about food as I am, his love of boxed macaroni and cheese still acts as reassurance that he wasn't coming for my parents' cooking after all. He'll be the first to confess that it was the chance to see me that kept him hanging around all those years ago.

Perhaps it was my openly cold shoulder, but my future husband decided to take a year off from college, join a Christian brotherhood in Europe and, if all went well, eventually become a monk. The day before he left I finally worked up the courage to tell him that maybe I did kind of maybe like him a little bit. But it was too late. We went our separate ways, staying in touch for the next five years with the occasional exchange of letters.

I finished my undergrad and Masters in Bioengineering in Arizona and enrolled in a PhD program in Neuroethics (a combination of bioethics and neuroscience) at McGill University in Montreal. I'd never lived anywhere but Phoenix, and Montreal was its opposite in every way. Snow to our sand, poutine to our chips and salsa – different weather, different culture, and a totally new circle of acquaintances. Up until my PhD program, I had lived either at home or close enough to home to never need to cook for myself. So, some 2500 miles from my parents' iconic culinary skills, I started to learn how to cook. I called home for recipes and techniques that I had never paid attention to before, but now found myself craving. I also had a copy of Kim Boyce's *Good to the Grain* and, because I could find all the unique flours in her recipes at the Jean Talon Market, I started baking my way through her book. Almost every Saturday I'd come home from the market with novel discoveries like fiddle leaves, rhubarb, buckwheat flour and chocolatine.

Two years into my program I received a letter out of the blue from my future-husband-almost-monk. He had decided not to become a lifelong brother after all, was moving home to Arizona, and wanted to reconnect. What I read between the lines was, 'Remember when you said you liked me? Want to give things a go?' In the five years since we'd parted ways I had dated other people, but I'd inevitably hold each one up to the bar that my college crush had set so long ago and eventually break up with the poor guy who was unknowingly trying to compete. His letter was the reopened door I didn't know I was hoping for. I wrote back and said *yes*.

Around the same time, other factors were pushing me away from the bitter cold and unexpected struggles in Montreal and pulling me towards home, family and the desert sun. After some hopeful long-distance conversations with my renewed love interest, I finally mustered up the courage to quit my PhD program and move home to Phoenix. Although I was glad to be back at the epic family dinner table, I was also overwhelmed by a sense of failure. The only job I could find was teaching evening cadaver labs at the community college, which didn't help with my feelings of humiliation, and, on top of that, picking up a relationship after five years apart was proving to be more difficult than either of us had expected.

When I wasn't teaching, I started helping my dad with this business venture, which was really just a glorified bread-baking hobby at the time, experimenting with baking in its simplest form – flour, yeast, water, salt. This led him to discover that using freshly milled flour made a stunning difference in the final product. He bought a 25 cm (10 inch) Meadows Mill (a small tabletop mill designed for the more serious hobbyist), which took up residence in the garage. He'd mill small bags of wheat, then ride his bicycle to deliver flour samples to local chefs. A Phoenix chef, Chris Bianco, had been looking for a source of local wheat for his James Beard Award–winning pizzeria. He and my dad got to scheming and struck a deal. With almost no experience under our belts, we immediately scaled up and ordered a 81 cm (32 inch) Osttiroler stone mill from Austria.

Chris gave us a small space at one of his restaurants, rent free, to set up the mill. I'm still not entirely sure what the terms of our arrangement were, but we had just enough room for our mill and one person.

ABOVE

With my family: Brian, Fitz, Sonora and Max.

On the day the mill arrived we had to dismantle the restaurant's back door to move it into place. That was August 13, 2011, and it marked the official starting date of Hayden Flour Mills, our homage to the local milling economy generated by Charles Hayden, whose mill had defined the commerce of Tempe, Arizona, and the surrounding valley from 1874 to 1998.

Those early days were couched in a golden haze of possibility and naiveté. But in reality, we had no customers and I discovered I was allergic to flour dust, so was in a constant state of red watery eyes and sniffles. Most distressingly of all – we had nothing to mill. We needed wheat seeds and a place to plant them. And then, even if we did have a source for local grain, our flour would cost three times as much as grocery store flour. So who would even buy it?

Finding wheat seeds turned out to be one of the most unexpected challenges of this whole project. We knew that if we were going to approach milling with such a radical commitment to craft, we needed to demonstrate equal care with what we actually milled. We'd honed in on some wheat varieties that used to be grown all across the country before the industrialization of agriculture, and one name came up over and over again: a heritage variety called White Sonora.

White Sonora was the first wheat that came to North America and was grown throughout Northern Mexico, Southern Arizona and Southern California for about 400 years. It was most likely one of the varieties Charles Hayden milled at the original Hayden Flour Mills in the late 1800s, but it had fallen out of favor over the last few decades and been replaced with modern, high-yield varieties. As intrigued as we were by this variety, it seemed impossible to find in any significant quantity besides small seed packets meant for home gardeners.

That is, until we got a call from someone who could not only get us White Sonora Wheat seed, but was the whole reason the seed was still in existence. In 1983 Gary Nabhan had founded a seed bank in Southern Arizona called Native Seeds/SEARCH, which had the foresight to bank arid-adapted crops of the Southwest, many of which were in danger of extinction. The story goes that a farmer had gifted Gary a coffee can filled with the last of his White Sonora seed, long ago set aside in favor of modern varieties. It ended up stored frozen in the Native Seeds/ SEARCH seed bank, patiently awaiting its resurgence.

Typically, seed banks exist to hold the genetic material of seeds for 'doomsday' scenarios, when we might need to access a genetic trait that would help make a crop more drought tolerant or stress resistant. It's more of a backup plan than nature's intended first choice, but, along with Native Seeds/SEARCH, we wanted to be part of a growing trend to repopulate our tables with these antiquated seeds.

Saving and replanting your own seeds is a little like your grandmother saving the tinfoil to reuse – it's cheap and resourceful and a little embarrassing. But as it turns out, Granny is on to something. As well as being a conscientious way to steward the earth's resources, saving our own seeds and replanting them in the same geographic area year after year causes a natural-selection process whereby the seed that succeeds is replanted and, over time, becomes naturally adapted to the climate and soil. We call these regionally adapted varietals 'landraces', and they are extremely important ecological players.

BELOW

The Sossaman Family on their farm in Queen Creek, Arizona. From left to right: Caroline, Steve and Chris.

A few years back we were asked to participate in a 'Get to know your food-maker' campaign at Whole Foods Market. I had to submit a headshot and a quote. I couldn't think of anything profound, so I spouted off something cheeky and figured I would change it later. Of course, I forgot, and a few months later I spotted my smiling face in the Whole Foods baking aisle saying, 'Unlike with animals, the best way to preserve endangered grains is to eat them!' I realize I am only compounding my embarrassment by repeating the statement here, and I'm still not sure whether my dry sense of humor translated to the wider public, but the point is simple: if we want to preserve biodiversity in our food system, we need to incorporate biodiversity at our tables. Unlike most worthwhile conservation work, it's not a hard job to eat these grains! It's probably one of the more hedonistic ways of saving our planet.

Of course this immediately begs the question: how does preserving grain diversity save the planet? And why do we need biodiversity in our food system at all? What is so bad about a monoculture? As with all living populations, genetic diversity prevents the total loss of a species through disease or disaster. Botanical variety is also essential for pollinators –

another threatened category in our ecology – by creating variety in their diet as well, meeting various needs for various species and colonies of bees, along with other crucial pollinators.

One of my personal values in preserving grain diversity is that it simply prevents boredom. Our wheat consumption in the States and throughout most of the world has been reduced to only four different categories of wheat, and the average American eats about 90 kg (200 lbs) of those flours a year. That's a lot of the same old thing over and over, and sadly we're impoverishing our experience of a vast food source that has been evolving for millennia. We knew there was a world of flavor, nutrients, textures and techniques waiting on the other side of reviving these forgotten grains, and we didn't see anyone else fighting for their survival. So we decided to do it ourselves.

With the help of Native Seeds/SEARCH we procured 450 kg (1000 lbs) of White Sonora seed. An old farmer friend of my dad's, Steve Sossaman, agreed to plant 10 acres of heritage wheat for us on the outer edges of Phoenix. That winter, just a few days before Christmas, we cut open sacks of White Sonora Wheat seed, filled the seeder, and planted our first crop. We said a blessing over the seed as it went into the field.

Later that summer, before we harvested the wheat, I walked into the field and gathered up a large bundle of this golden bounty. That bundle would become my wedding bouquet five months later, and this intoxicating wheat would define the next decade of my life.

We knew that if we were going to approach milling with such a detailed attention and radical commitment to craft, we needed to demonstrate equal care with what we actually milled.

GROW

'STICKERS ON THE CONTRARY ARE MOTIVATED BY AFFECTION,
BY SUCH LOVE FOR A PLACE AND ITS LIFE THAT THEY WANT TO
PRESERVE IT AND REMAIN IN IT.'
Wendell Berry

About two years into starting the mill, a then-popular American website featured our mill on their homepage. Under a photo of my dad standing in a field of White Sonora Wheat was the click-bait heading, 'Arizona man claims this heritage wheat will feed the world'. Despite the largest influx of online orders for our White Sonora Flour we had ever seen, we had a good laugh about this overblown headline. At the time the article was published, we only had about 100 acres of wheat in production: enough wheat to feed our friends, plus a few more. Certainly not the world.

Not that long ago there *was* a man who claimed his wheat could feed the world, and in 1970 he was awarded a Nobel Prize for saving one billion people from starvation. His name was Norman Borlaug. His groundbreaking work in wheat breeding sparked what has come to be known as the 'Green Revolution'. He crossed dwarf wheat with rust-resistant wheats and ended up increasing wheat yields by six times. It was as if he condensed 10,000 years of progress in gently domesticating wheat into ten years of research. These new wheat seeds were like real-life beans from Jack's magical Giant Beanstalk.

Farmers didn't waste any time putting aside their timeworn seeds and implementing these new wheat varieties. In Mexico, where Norman Borlaug developed the new varieties, the farmers fed their own people, avoiding impending famine, and began to export their excess. Increasing yields did indeed help to create more food per acre, but, as with all the best laid plans, it had ripples of unforeseen consequences. Farms were forced to scale up while chasing larger and larger yields to stay competitive in a global market. The new wheats encouraged

> If we completely dismiss
> older wheat varieties, we lose
> things like soil health, nutrient
> density, genetic resilience and,
> most importantly, the foodways
> surrounding these foods.

monocultures (the exclusive planting of one variety), which are more susceptible to being wiped out en masse by new strains of disease such as stem rusts. Farmers scrambled to manage their increased dependence on inputs like fertilizers and pesticides, not to mention the urgency of seed companies continually putting out the latest and greatest seed model. Just as most of us are at the mercy of the latest operating system to stay relevant in our tech-hungry world, farmers were suddenly expected to chase an always-moving target of up-to-date seed technology.

To put these advances in perspective, one of Borlaug's star wheat varieties, Sonora64, could produce over 2700 kg (6000 lbs) of harvested wheat per acre. White Sonora Wheat, one of the heritage varieties that we have worked to revive, produces half of that. Unsurprisingly, that also means that our White Sonora will also be twice as expensive, since every farmer still needs to get the same profit margin from their acre of land.

The Green Revolution sparked a seismic shift in wheat farming, and the flour and bread you buy at the grocery store are marked by this revolution every step of the way from seed to bread. It takes as many as 109 chemicals to get through the process of planting, growing, harvesting, milling and baking with commercial wheat – from amending the depleted soil, killing weeds and pests, fumigating the grain silos, to fortifying the flour and conditioning the dough. By contrast, the wheat we grow and mill uses zero.

Our mill focuses on processing heritage and ancient grains. We define heritage (or heirloom) grains as wheat varieties that existed before the onset of the Green Revolution of the 1960s. Ancient grains, which include einkorn and farro, are defined as being thousands of years old – the ancestors of modern wheats.

So why would we undo this incredible agricultural Nobel Prize–winning progress and choose to return to pre-1970s varieties of wheat? Why would we trade this humanitarian panacea for lower yields, higher prices, greater risks of crop losses, and grain varieties that have had almost no market demand?

It is not to diminish the role of traditional plant breeding, selection, hybridization and technology in improving agriculture. But if we completely dismiss these older wheat varieties we lose things like soil health, nutrient density, genetic resilience and, most importantly, the foodways surrounding these foods. These grains might not feed the world, but we'd like to think we're doing a good job of feeding our community and re-localizing our food systems.

White Sonora Wheat and all the products we make from it have consistently been our top sellers. This has always baffled us because, while it is full of flavor, it can be a bit tricky to work with. It doesn't give you big fluffy loaves of white bread or big airy European hearth breads. I think our customers simply like the fact that their flour comes from somewhere and someone, and has a story rooted in the Southwest.

This is how it all started, and along the way, we've added other grains to our collection, meeting new seeds, learning their stories, and advocating for their preservation by way of use.

I remember our first large order for chickpea flour, weighing out each bag by hand and closing them with our foot-powered heat sealer. I carefully applied the labels my cousin had designed as a school project, which I'd printed on my home inkjet printer. On delivery, I received a crisp $500 check. Since then we've had many large orders that dwarf that amount, but I have never felt the same satisfaction and pride that I did with that first significant order. We started getting calls from local chefs and boutique markets and had a modest business on our hands. Soon we were able to hire our first employee: a miller. We hired an eager young man named Benjamin Butler, and he began learning the ins and outs of our mill and grains from scratch. Armed with a full-time miller and a new sense of confidence, we expanded our reach and began pursuing opportunities for greater exposure.

I was sitting in the parking lot of a Discount Tire shop waiting on a replacement for yet another busted tire on our work truck when the editor of *Martha Stewart Living* magazine called and told me we had won the Martha Stewart American Made contest. The prize included a trip to New York, a $10,000 cash prize, a feature in her magazine and a professionally filmed brand video. The video crew would be heading our way in two weeks. I got off the phone and my excitement turned into a cold sweat. What no one knew, except me, my dad and the miller, was that our mill was currently homeless.

We had outgrown our space in the back of the restaurant and long outstayed our welcome. The mill produced so much dust that we were constantly overburdening the air-conditioning filters, and the health department was beginning to ask questions about our unconventional arrangement. We had started the process of moving out to the farm

We use the rose from the historic
Hayden Flour Mills' iconic Arizona
Rose Flour bag on our modern boxes.

THE MILLER'S DAUGHTER

where most of our wheat was grown – our farmer partner had generously offered to remodel a barn for us – but the space wouldn't be ready for at least another six months. In the meantime, we were taking refuge in the corner of a friend's electrical parts warehouse. We hung temporary plastic walls and tried to leave minimal flour tracks in our wake. Our friend's generosity certainly kept us afloat, but I didn't want anyone to see this humble set-up, let alone a video crew from *Martha Stewart Living*.

In the end the video crew did their 'movie magic' and made it appear that we were in our new location rather than the dark corner of a warehouse. I still think of this time as the 'dark ages' of our business. I'm glad we stubbornly carried on; the exposure generated by the award was worth far more than the prize money and would propel us into a period of rapid growth. We moved into our new on-farm location, and it was time for our business to grow up.

We won a USDA (United States Department of Agriculture) grant and were able to properly update our branding. Inspired by the historic mill, we developed the bright packaging that we are still known for. To increase our production, we added a second mill. My dad and little brother restored a 76 cm (30 inch) American-made Meadows Mill and painted it bright yellow. (It has since found a new home at a mill in California.) We continued with our grain restoration efforts, adding two pasta wheats from Iraq, a Tibetan Purple Barley, Gazelle Rye and einkorn. We added three types of pancake mix and heritage grain crackers to our product line. We started working with distributors, delivering entire pallets at a time instead of a few cases; I no longer drove the truck all over Arizona every Friday to hand-deliver our products. Orders got larger and we found ourselves in the spotlight.

We outgrew our new space within a year of moving into it, making it necessary to build a new facility on the farm with enough room to house our partner farmer's brand-new grain cleaning equipment. Another big step forward for us, as we no longer had to clean our grain on equipment held together by duct tape. We won another USDA grant, which enabled us to purchase a built-to-specification stone mill from Italy. We realized we had become a full-blown business, championing a real cause, and it was starting to gather momentum, whether we were ready or not. Throughout all of this, my dad kept his day job and I had to learn the ins and outs of running a business, something academia had not prepared me for. I was able to hire a few more employees, which was especially welcome as my husband and I were expecting our first baby.

We had come through our darkest days at the mill, charging full throttle towards the light at the end of the tunnel after years of cobbling together solutions and resources.

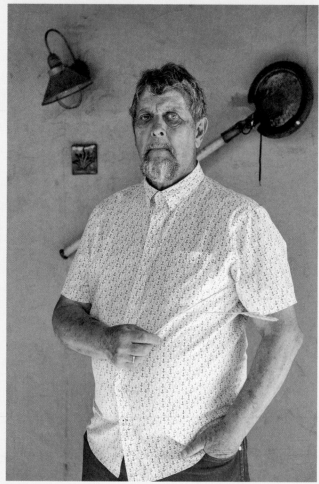

ABOVE

A portrait of Gary Nabhan at his
home in Southern Arizona. Gary
has been a champion of the local
food movement in Arizona and the
Borderlands. He helped us locate
our first White Sonora seeds.

RIGHT

My dad taking a break during harvest
before a summer storm rolls in.

24   THE MILLER'S DAUGHTER

I think our customers simply like the fact that their flour comes from somewhere and someone, and has a story rooted in the Southwest.

HARVEST

'EVERYWHERE THE GRAIN STOOD RIPE AND THE HOT AFTERNOON
WAS FULL OF THE SMELL OF THE RIPE WHEAT, LIKE THE SMELL
OF BREAD BAKING IN AN OVEN.'
Willa Cather, *O Pioneers!*

From January until March, I worry about our crops. They look so short this year. The alfalfa is coming back up and will surely choke out our wheat – just stubby little tufts of grass struggling to emerge from the desert floor. I'm convinced that this is the year the crops will fail and we will have to close our doors. But without fail, the first day of spring brings a glimmer of hope. The wheat heads begin to poke out from the broad blades of grass, and I breathe a sigh of relief. Over the next few weeks, the wheat will triple in size and all will be well.

Towards the end of March, our wheat fields start looking like wheat fields. One day they are just fields of green grass and the next day the stems shoot up above the first node, and slender heads of wheat emerge from the flag leaf. Towards the end of April, I can almost watch the fields ripen before my eyes: turning from green to yellow, the tips of their awns blackening in the Phoenix sun.

By the end of May, the field of Blue Beard Durum is so tall it covers my head. I walk in as far as I dare and stand on my toes and peek out over the top of the wheat heads. I watch the wheat heads sway in the wind. The next day, when I return, this field has been bent over by the wind, flattened and matted. It will be a minor pain at harvest, but I wish you could have been there for that one brief day when the field looked like a tumultuous desert ocean.

My favorite field of late is the Tibetan Purple Barley. It's waist high and, as I walk through it, I can run my hands over the soft heads that are just starting to turn purple. The heads of this variety of barley are petite and cylindrical, very different from the wide fat heads of the durum with its spiky awns.

ABOVE

A combine cutting a field of White
Sonora Wheat.

Even though the fields are surrounded by new subdivisions to the west
and north, our wheat fields attract their own ecosystem. While checking
on the crops early one morning, I see hundreds of soldier birds with their
bright red epaulets, a snowy egret, a pair of desert cottontails, a quail
family, and ground squirrels fleeing as they hear the rustle of my footsteps.

This year, the farro is struggling. We are trying a new variety that sheds
its hull more easily, but it's coming up in patches and looks sad next to
the field of Bronze Barley next door, standing straight and tall with
bright yellow heads that catch into flame at sunset.

When my dad and I first started the mill I had the romantic idea that half
my days would be spent in this way – frolicking through the wheat fields

THE MILLER'S DAUGHTER

Without fail, every year we declare it the best loaf we've ever had and therefore the best harvest yet!

and chasing cottontails. The other half would be milling and baking with the freshly milled flour. I forgot the part where I climb a step ladder and try to dump 22 kg (50 lbs) buckets of grain over my head and into the mill's hopper. And the part where I run marketing and payroll and operations and try to make a living selling obscure stone-ground flours. These days, I only get to mill when our miller goes on vacation, and even as I struggle to lift the bags of flour and count the days until he returns, I think he has the best job in the world. This is the kind of job that people chained to their desks daydream about. Now that our mill is located on the farm where we grow the wheat I try to stop at the fields as much as I can, but it's never as often as I'd like.

When summer temperatures peak around mid-July, the wheat begins to dry out in the field and turn a toasted amber. The wheat stalks shrink by half and bend over in submission to the sun. Since our acreage is small compared with most wheat growers, we have to beg the combiner to squeeze us in. We are often their last stop before they leave the state and head through the heartland, harvesting their way from Arizona to Canada. Harvest is less like Millet's *The Angelus* and more like Van Gogh's *Resting in the Hay* as we take turns napping in the shade to avoid sun stroke. It's long days in the scorching heat, tagging in and out of the fields and taking turns filling giant tote bags with the grain that shoots straight out of the combine like a fire hose.

I hitch a ride on the combine (not just to avoid work, although the cabs of most modern combines are well air-conditioned) and check out the stats coming up on the dash. The yield and moisture are all calculated in real time.

Harvest is a brutal but beautiful time filled with excitement. We say things like, 'The White Sonora is so much more golden this year', 'Look at these plump Red Fife berries, they're so much bigger than last year's crop' and 'Can you believe the yields on this Blue Beard Durum? I think it likes the desert.' But it's an all-hands-on-deck test of survival. We take a break from our heritage grain diet and subsist on gas station food and cold watermelon.

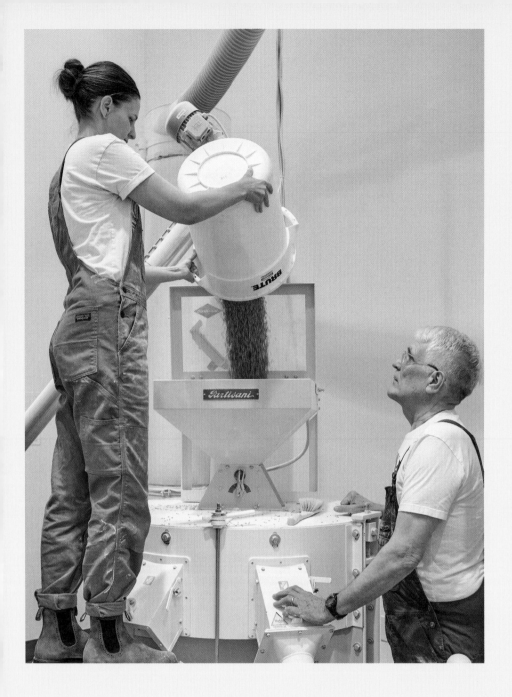

ABOVE

My dad and me filling the hopper of the mill with einkorn in preparation to make flour. The granite stone is completely encased by the white metal cover.

RIGHT

Admiring the Red Fife Wheat as it comes out of the field.

THE MILLER'S DAUGHTER

When all the grain has been brought in, we begin to stress about a new problem – cleaning. The wheat that comes straight from the field is filled with weed seeds, chaff, dirt clods, rocks and bits of wheat stalk. Again, we have to beg the big guys to squeeze us in and run our pittance of dirty grain through their big screens and fans. It's always a time-sensitive matter as our barns are empty and we have orders to fill.

But before it goes to the cleaners, we pull off a portion of some of the grain and clean it by hand. Our miller mills it up and we bake it into a loaf of first fruits as an act of gratitude. Without fail, every year we declare it the best loaf we've ever had and therefore the best harvest yet!

MILL

'TRULY TRULY I SAY TO YOU, UNLESS A GRAIN OF WHEAT FALLS INTO
THE GROUND AND DIES, IT ABIDES ALONE. BUT IF IT DIES, IT BEARS
MUCH FRUIT.'
John 12:24

'll let you in on a little industry secret. When you go to the grocery store and see all the different brands of flour on the shelf, those bags are almost certainly filled with the same type of flour from the same mill, sourced from one of the few large-scale industrial mills in the US.

When we first started the mill, one of our favorite statistics to quote was a snippet of information my dad found in a historical government document. It goes like this: in 1874 there were 24,000 mills in the US; by 1982 there were fewer than 200 mills, and 80 percent of those mills were owned by just six larger companies. This stat would always make quite an impression. People would get sad, like we were talking about an endangered species, and in some ways we were. The loss of small mills correlated directly to the loss of biodiversity in wheat varieties.

I'd been running Hayden Flour Mills for eight years before I had the chance to visit one of these large-scale mills, also known as an industrial roller mill. It was a modern marvel – the flour going up and down a six-story building, transported through a maze of blue pipes. Razor-sharp rollers, scourers, hula-hooping sifters, purifiers, color sorters, temperers ... no wonder you need a university degree to operate such a mill. To train our miller, we handed him the three-page manual that came with our Austrian stone mill. It was in German. He didn't speak German, but to be fair, it had quite a few helpful pictures. Over time, our miller refined his craft and became quite skilled, learning to dress the stone, replace the sifter screens, and mill corn, wheat and beans on our little wooden mill.

Stone milling is a very simple technology compared with roller milling and has remained virtually unchanged since the first century, powered by everything from humans to animals, water, steam, wind, electricity and, in our case, solar power. A stationary stone sits under a matching stone that rotates on top. The stones are carved with thin patterned lines called furrows. As the grain flows into the furrows from the hopper above, it is broken open; the separated elements of the grain fall apart and are pushed to the outer edge of the stone as whole wheat flour. At our mill, we often add a secondary process of bolting or sifting the grain, which is also a historical practice, although we use a more efficient technique than sifting it by hand through a cloth as Sarah from the Old Testament story did to make fine cakes for visiting angels. Sifting removes different amounts of the bran and germ. It's an imprecise process by design, so no matter how finely we sift (say for a pastry flour) we always end up with pieces of the whole grain in the final product, which only enhances the flavor and nutrition.

Industrial roller mills were introduced to the United States in the 1880s, designed to efficiently separate all three parts of the grain – germ, bran and endosperm. A perfectly white substance made only from endosperm became the flour that the industrial food system is built on. And modern wheat was bred specifically for roller milling and industrial bread, with uniform size and moisture, thick bran coatings and high levels of protein. In fact, roller milling is so efficient at separating the endosperm of the grain that it becomes almost entirely nutritionally void and has to be chemically enriched with iron, folic acid, riboflavin, niacin and thiamine. If you start paying close attention to food labels, you will see these ingredients listed over and over again in association with 'flour'. It seems a bit nonsensical to remove the naturally occurring nutrition from flour and then reintroduce it from other sources. But this practice created an infinitely shelf-stable food – the gold standard in an industrialized and globalized food system.

In one day, an industrial roller mill can mill over 450,000 kg (1,000,000 lbs) of grain. In one day, we mill 2700 kg (6000 lbs) of grain on our stone mill. To put that in perspective, it would take us eight months to achieve the output of just one day in an industrial mill. In ancient times, it would take a Roman soldier an hour to convert his ration of wheat to 4.5 kg (10 lbs) of flour on a saddle stone – a wide flat mortar and pestle. Across many cultures and ages, bread has been considered sacred. In reality, a loaf of bread is a tangible manifestation of many hours of laboring to sow, harvest, thresh, mill, leaven and bake, the efforts of many members of a community coming together in a physical object which then feeds the broader society.

I could probably make a good argument that stone-milled flour is objectively better than roller-milled flour, but I'm going to leave it at the fact that they are just two different ways of making flour. I will tell you that we were attracted to stone milling, not just because of its romantic

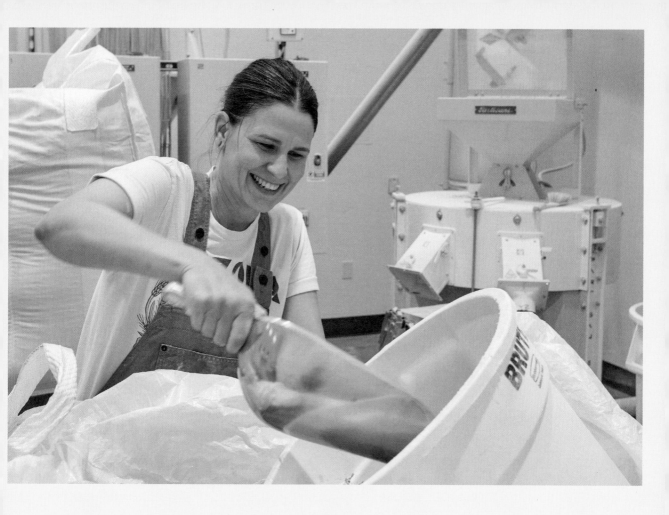

Miller's assistant Alison Gillis mixing White Sonora pancake mix and getting it ready to go into retail boxes.

simplicity, but because of the nutritional wholeness that brings about an intensity of flavor that industrial milled flour doesn't have. Even when we sift or bolt our flours, stone milling is natural and simple enough that parts of the bran and germ (the real flavor powerhouse of the grain) are still present in the end product. Stone milling also seems like a gentler match for these heritage and ancient grains that haven't been bred for the rigors of the big-time mills.

When I first set out to help my dad with his milling hobby, I could never have predicted that in ten years, I would still be spending my days and evenings weighing in on problems at the mill or booking speaking engagements on the societal significance of food processing. I never dreamed I'd still be involved in grain development and milling through all my personal transitions of moving, dating, engagement, marriage, pregnancy, becoming a mother, then a mother of two, then a mother of three. As each new season arose, the mill quietly followed me into the developing chapter with its challenges and demands.

When I had my first baby, I expected to weather the change just as I had all the changes that came before it. I gave myself what I thought was a generous maternity leave of six weeks. And then after those six weeks, I jumped back into running the mill as if nothing had changed and without any kind of childcare. It worked for a while, while my son was a small sleepy newborn, until it didn't work. I was more than a little surprised when I was going about my day and suddenly thought I was having a heart attack, believed I was dying, and went straight to the hospital. I eventually came to find out that I was suffering my first panic attack. Apparently, this is not uncommon after having a baby, another reality in league with miscarriages and pelvic floor dysfunction in the category of widely shared experiences that are not openly discussed. That is, until it happened to me, and then it seemed like everyone I knew was happy to share their stories of postpartum ER visits and favorite antidepressants.

When I was pregnant, I had prepared myself by reading a popular French parenting book and had the notion that after the baby arrived, life would continue on as it had but with a baby strapped to me in his carrier, along for the ride. The same life as before but with a cute little baby accessory. The only part of this that proved to be true was the baby being in his carrier, since being strapped to me was the only place where he'd stop crying hysterically.

Becoming a mother is indeed a kind of grinding not unlike the transformation of our heritage grains. I too was being cracked and spilled open. All my parts unfolded, and my heart especially exposed. These small helpless people that call me Mom, a constant reminder that we are all just floury dust and to dust we shall return. And yet, somehow,

THE MILLER'S DAUGHTER

Persisting became a matter
of stubborn pride but also
conviction.

ABOVE

Head miller Diego Madueno in the
ripened White Sonora fields.

38   THE MILLER'S DAUGHTER

I found my own small furrow and followed it back out into the world transformed and healed. It took many false starts and re-tries to find the right balance of work and motherhood, but eventually a combination of hiring a general manager, longer maternity leaves, childcare and therapy helped me find my footing again.

I don't mean to say that I have found the magical answer to 'having it all'. Even this cookbook was mostly written and tested with one arm as I nursed, bounced or consoled one of my three children. It's not the most straightforward way to work, and I have lots of help from family, various childcare arrangements, and a small reliable team that runs the day-to-day workings of the mill. Working this way is slow and less efficient, but I don't think I would enjoy it any other way – it is intentionally slow, which also happens to be how we mill our flour and make our food.

My husband and I often say that all the university degrees and exotic world travels we devoted ourselves to in our twenties pale in comparison to the enrichment of becoming parents. It's a surprising thing to admit considering what a difficult adjustment it has been and how much we gripe about how hard parenting is. All I know is that I very much love nurturing the mill and my little family, and just like stone milling, I'm drawn to the less precise, less efficient, less sterile process of trying to juggle all these relationships and work. I'd rather be present to all of them imperfectly.

I am very proud of our successes, but behind us is a heavy trail of failed endeavors, false starts and hardships. We sold White Sonora Flour lavash bread at the farmers' market for a brief stint, we helped start a bagel program with the Phoenix Rescue Mission, we dabbled with the idea of producing barley water, we got deep into the development of a pickled grain product (yes I know, very unappetizing), I made custom mesquite polenta boards for a while, we experimented with milling grape skin flour, we tried to make a roasted green wheat called freekeh with a refugee farmer, but in the end we harvested the crop too late. We've had our share of pest-eaten crops, spilled totes of grain, missed payrolls, non-paying customers, broken equipment and opportunities that never panned out. In sum, a million reasons to quit. But I decided a long time ago that if the business failed, I would feign gluten intolerance rather than go back to eating industrial wheat. Persisting became a matter of stubborn pride but also conviction. Conviction that these grains and flours really are better for our bodies and the soil, and that they really do taste that much better than the average bag of white flour.

COOKING NOTES

I like to hide puns and silly phrases all over our packaging. On the inside flap of one of our flour boxes is the suggestion to 'Take time to smell the fresh flours'. It's there to make people smile, but I also hope our customers really do as they're told, stick their noses deep into the bag, and take in the aroma of the flour that they have just opened. Working with freshly milled flours is a sensory experience, from the fragrance to the color to the feel of the flour. Occasionally, I find myself stuck without any Hayden Flour Mills flour and have to grab an industrially milled bag at the grocery store. Every time, I am blown away by the difference between our flour and this chalky white substance. As well as being highly aromatic, freshly milled flour is silky and luscious. When you squeeze some in your fist and release it, the flour holds the imprint of your fingers. This is due to the oils from the bran and germ giving it a phantom feeling of moisture. If you spread the flour thinly over your palm and look closely, you'll see the hallmark of stone-milled flour – golden flecks of bran. Before we receive a new tote (a giant 905 kg/2000 lb sack) of grain at the mill, we open it and give it a close inspection. Running our hands through the kernels is addictively soothing, as we look for discoloration or shriveled kernels. And then we always smell it, to make sure it smells like wheat and only wheat.

Before we begin, I feel obliged to give you fair warning: if the only grain ingredient you've ever heard about has been a bag of white bleached and enriched all-purpose (plain) flour from the grocery store, you may become a little overwhelmed by all the information about heritage flours and grains. There are so many different kinds of grains!

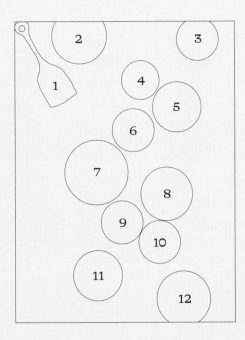

LEFT

1 – Chickpea Flour
2 – White Sonora Wheat Berries
3 – Purple Barley Flour
4 – Farro Berries
5 – Polenta
6 – Red Fife Wheat Berries
7 – Oats
8 – Bronze & Purple Barley Berries
9 – Rye Berries
10 – Einkorn Berries
11 – Chickpeas
12 – Blue Beard Durum Berries

The United States Department of Agriculture (USDA) seed bank houses 500 varieties of wheat. And that doesn't include the many other kinds of grains they hold, some with familiar names and some completely obscure. Then, within each variety of grain, the harvested seed can be used in a wide range of transformations, including whole berry form, sprouted, cracked, malted, or milled into flour or meal.

In this book, I'm highlighting nine varieties of grain and one legume. By the end of our adventure, you'll be well equipped to work with any one of them in your own home kitchen. Up until now you may have been coloring with a small packet of basic crayons – I'm about to give you the deluxe box, with a dozen shades of red. It may seem a bit much at first, but stay with me; your works of art will be so much richer for it.

Don't worry if you're not ready for a deep dive into the vast world of grains; you're in good company. This book just gives you the chance to dip your toes in the water. The variations in these more unusual types of grains can make them tricky to work with, but those same variations are what make them so special and yield such beautiful results. My recipes are extremely forgiving (you'll find no artisan bread recipes here) and don't feature any of the technical jargon elite bakers love to nerd out on, like protein percentages or ash contents or baker's math. Instead, I offer simple ways to begin working with these grains, with results that are so delicious you'll soon be hooked on the spectrum of flavors and dishes now open to you.

My goal is to make this book universal to the Small Grain Revival, so, for instance, you can pick up some fresh milled polenta from any local mill and make Pink Polenta (see page 149). There's plenty of room for variation in most of my recipes, and I made sure to test them using different brands of grains. For the most accurate results, I do recommend that you use a kitchen scale. Even if my mill and your neighborhood mill do things a bit differently, our scales will always match up.

I've included alternative names for different flours, as well as other types of heritage grains that make a good substitute if you can't find the variety specified in the recipe. I've also included a resource section (page 220) for finding mills across North America, the UK, Australia and New Zealand that carry heritage and ancient grains or quality stone-milled flours. When we started Hayden Flour Mills, there were only a handful of small mills in the US. To our great joy, it seems there is now a local grain economy in nearly every state. So many of these mills are run by friends, wonderful passionate people. We'd be so happy if this book inspired you to seek them out and support their efforts.

So all you need to do now is enter this wonderful world of grain variety and be willing to make a few mistakes. Ask your local miller questions (they will be very happy to talk to you!), and maybe pick just one new variety to start with. You will soon get the hang of it. When I started milling, I was constantly asking my dad to confirm which grain was which so I didn't deliver the wrong product. Now, I could identify each variety by how it looks in the field, subtle differences in grain size and

LEFT

From top to bottom: Purple Barley
Flour, White Sonora Type 00 Flour,
Semolina Flour, Rye Flour.

color, the smell when it's slightly damp and the flavor of the flour.
They are as different to me as each of my children.

Each grain has its strengths and weaknesses. Once, one of our chef
partners said very poetically while standing in the middle of our first
wheat field: 'We will let the wheat tell us what it wants to be.' Some
bakers use protein numbers and falling numbers to determine what a
grain should become, but I prefer to go about it more intuitively. I take
the same approach with my recipes: they are simple by design to bring
out the innate characteristics of each grain and highlight its unique
flavor profile.

ABOVE

Sprouting Rye and Purple Barley
Berries. The small white tails
indicate they are ready.

THE MILLER'S DAUGHTER

CRACKED GRAINS

Softer grains like White Sonora, rye, einkorn and oat groats can be cracked in a high-speed blender. They generally just need a few pulses at high speed.

HOW TO SPROUT GRAINS

Sprouting brings out the sweetness of the grain and changes the nutritional profile. Rye, White Sonora, einkorn, oats and barley all sprout very easily.

In a quart glass jar (about 950 ml), cover 1 cup of grain in water, cover the jar, and leave to soak for 12 hours. Drain and rinse the grain, then drain again.

Replace the jar's lid with something permeable that will allow the water to drain but not the grain. Cheesecloth (muslin) secured with a rubber band is my preference. Place the jar upside down in a bowl at a 45-degree angle. This will keep the grain from collecting water and allow air to circulate. Rinse and drain the grains every 8–12 hours.

Every grain takes a different amount of time to start sprouting, but it generally takes 48 hours. When they have tiny white tails sprouting, rinse them and cook them until tender and chewy. Sprouted grains can be stored in the fridge for 1–3 days until you are ready to use them. Always cook sprouted grains before using them in a recipe.

HYDRATION

You'll notice that many of the doughs in this book have high hydration rates. This is because our desert grains are dry and thirsty. If you acquire your grains from a wetter region, they may require less hydration. Please don't hesitate to adjust the recipe by adding more liquid or more flour as needed; just do it in small increments so you don't end up overcorrecting. Sometimes, 1–2 teaspoons of flour or liquid (in some recipes this is in the form of butter) is all the dough needs. Over time you'll develop an intuition for the feel of a perfectly hydrated dough.

We allow our grains to dry in the field before harvest; they sit out baking in the summer sun until all the crops are ready to harvest. In wetter regions, like the Northeast, growers harvest their grains and then have to dry them with large fans so they don't become moldy. Our Southwest grains will have 8.5–9% moisture levels at harvest, and Northeastern grains will be closer to 12%. I see these different moisture levels in flours and grains as a way to connect to where your grains come from.

You will also notice a range of moisture levels when cooking whole grains, but the solution is to treat whole grains like pasta and taste as you go, adjusting the time as required. As a general rule, lower-moisture grains will take longer to cook. I have provided cooking times that work well for me using our Arizona grains, but things might look a bit different in your kitchen, so be flexible and use your intuition.

KITCHEN ESSENTIALS

These kitchen appliances are not absolutely essential; they are just some of the things that bring me joy in the kitchen. Not having every last thing should not prevent you from getting busy in the kitchen. Just make a start with what you have.

KITCHEN TOOLS

- rimmed baking sheets or trays
- parchment (baking) paper or silicone baking mats
- beeswax wraps
- spatulas
- wooden spoons
- spider strainer
- rolling pin
- gnocchi board
- kitchen scale (10 lbs/4.5 kg limit)
- microplane
- mixing bowls
- bench scraper
- oven thermometer
- mortar and pestle
- sharp knives

APPLIANCES

Stand mixer: A good-quality stand mixer can be pricey. Since food is my job, I have invested in a stand mixer and it is the workhorse of my kitchen, but I do want to be clear that it's not a required tool. Any time I use a stand mixer in the recipes, you can achieve the same results with a wooden spoon and good old-fashioned elbow grease. When a recipe calls for 'creaming' egg/sugar/butter, you can simply use a handheld electric beater.

High-speed blender: A high-speed blender can double as a small flour mill for softer grains like oats and einkorn. It can also be used to crack grains, which can shorten cooking times and add texture to dishes. Some blender brands even sell special attachments for grinding some of the harder wheats into whole wheat flours. A blender comes in handy for so many other applications, and it's one of the few appliances that lives on my counter and never gets put away.

Pasta roller: Again, not a necessity, but this is a tool I really enjoy using. It makes recipes for fresh pasta or very thin crackers one step less intimidating. It's also fun for a communal cooking event and I've lent it to neighbors enough times to make it worthwhile.

Electric pressure cooker: This appliance helps me cook from scratch, but what I really love about it is that I can cook dinner and sneak in a power nap at the same time, something I might not attempt if I had a pot of grains cooking on the stove. An electric pressure cooker just adds that small layer of convenience that makes whole wheat berries and dried beans much less intimidating.

MEASURING FLOUR BY WEIGHT AND VOLUME

As I mentioned before, the most important kitchen gadget you'll need for these recipes is a kitchen scale. Your best chance of success is cooking from weight, so please give it a try.

Take time to smell
the fresh flours.

Freshly milled flour is tricky because it varies in density, and this
makes measuring with cups very inconsistent. However, if all you have
available to you is a set of cups, this is how I recommend measuring
your flour:

> Scoop the flour into a measuring cup, then tap the bottom of the cup
> on the counter to settle the flour. This tapping method removes some
> of the air in the flour but doesn't pack it down.

> Fill up any remaining space in the cup with flour and scrape the top
> with a knife edge to remove any excess.

Because flours vary so much from mill to mill and even according to
the weather, I've tried to provide as many visual clues as possible to
help you adjust the recipe in your own kitchen, adding more flour or
moisture to achieve the right consistency.

OAT FLOUR

Because oat groats are so soft, they can easily be cracked or turned into flour in a blender with no special milling equipment.

To make oat flour, blitz the oat groats for 60 seconds in a blender at high speed. Because oats are naturally very oily, the heat of the blender can cause the flour to gum up, so take care not to let the flour heat up too much. Don't worry about making a super-fine flour; in fact, a coarse texture will improve most recipes.

OVEN

All the recipes in this book were made using a conventional oven. If you are using a convection (fan-forced) oven, reduce the temperature by 14°C (25°F).

PEARLED VERSUS UNPEARLED (OR WHOLE) GRAINS

It is common to find pearled barley and pearled farro at the grocery store. This simply means the hard outer layer has been polished off and therefore the grain requires a shorter cooking time. If the pearled variety is all you can find, follow the directions on the packet rather than the cooking time given in the recipe.

I prefer my whole grains unpearled because they have more bite, but the best grain is the one you can easily find. Both types will work well.

RAW DOUGH

This is the official, legal disclaimer not to eat anything with raw flour in it. Snitch cookie dough at your own risk.

RINSING

A quick rinse is a must for whole grains before cooking.

SOAKING

If you're just getting started as a cook, skip the soak. It's just another barrier or potential excuse. As you gain more experience and even start enjoying your time in the kitchen, layer in the step of soaking. It makes a small, nuanced difference to the end product. And personally, I like the ritual of soaking grains. Setting out a bowl of soaking farro the night before sends me to bed with visions of all the delicious things I will make the next day.

STORAGE

Let's talk about bugs. I'm sure this topic will get me banned from ever writing another cookbook, but I've been dying to get this taboo topic out in the open. I used to turn my nose up at bugs. Years ago at summer camp, when I discovered the cook had been sifting weevils from the flour bin, I skipped the peach cobbler for the rest of the week.

But here's the thing: bugs, birds and ground squirrels all love grain, and the fewer chemicals you put on your grain the tastier it will be for these field critters. It's a matter of picking your battles, so I've learned to embrace the critters, though we don't let them run rampant. In fact, we devote a lot of energy to safe and natural bug control.

I've learned to look at the bug problem from a different angle – if these critters don't want to eat your grain, maybe they know something we don't. Maybe they know that modern industrial wheat is grown with a ton of chemicals and that industrial grain silos are fumigated regularly. It's like my dog, who eats everything my children drop on the floor (including rocks), but won't touch their breakfast cereal. It just makes you wonder what it's made of.

The way the bugs end up in our grain and flour is actually quite fascinating. They hide their microscopic larvae on the grain while it is developing, then, when conditions are right, they hatch and are born into an endless source of food. The bugs are essentially stowaways in our sacks of grain! And they have been clever little nuisances for thousands of years – munching away on even the Pharaoh's grain stores. (Think fascinating, not gross.)

Over the years, we have found this amazing all-natural way to cut down on bugs by removing the oxygen from our grain bins. Without an oxygen supply, the bugs can't hatch and the larvae only exist in miniscule amounts.

When storing flours and grains in your kitchen, keep them tightly sealed. If you have room in your freezer, store them there as your flours will stay fresh, and the sub-zero temperatures will kill any potential stowaways. If you do find a few bugs in your grain and it hasn't become an infestation (at which point, it's chicken food), I recommend putting the flour or grain in the freezer for 24 hours and then sifting the bugs out. Use your senses as a guide – spoiled grain will have an acidic or ammonia-like scent.

So the lesson here is don't be afraid of a few little bugs. It means your flour is the real deal! But do follow my advice for proper storage. And of course, if you bought the flour or grain from me, I'll happily replace it for you if it doesn't smell or look right.

STORAGE OF COOKED GRAINS

Store cooked grains in their cooking liquid in the fridge for one week. Grains that have already been used in a salad will only last a day or two as the salt in the dressing will draw out the moisture and start to make them overly chewy.

TO NOTE

This book uses 240 ml (8 fl oz) cup measures and 15 ml (½ fl oz) tablespoon measures. Australian and British cooks should be scant in their cup measures.

WHITE SONORA

When I moved to Montréal in 2009 to start my PhD program, I packed a rice cooker, cans of chipotles and green chilies in case I could not find spicy food in French Canada, my collection of T.S. Eliot poems and Willa Cather novels, and a pair of snow boots that a friend had passed along. I never read the books, hardly used the rice cooker and ended up becoming so immersed in the Quebecois food culture that I forgot all about my need for chilies. In the end, the bulky snow boots were the only thing that actually came in handy.

In modern days, packing a suitcase of food seems impractical, but in the 1600s it was not uncommon, and indeed very practical, to travel with seeds and plants from home. This is how wheat made its way to what is now known as North America, as the legend goes, brought in the pockets of Padre Lorenzo de Cardenas on a boat from Spain around 1640. It's more likely that many varieties of soft white wheats were brought over by different Jesuit missionaries as they made the voyage from Spain and Germany to their American mission assignments, not only providing the needed means to make bread for the Eucharist but also carrying those foreign evangelists through their voluntary exile with the familiar food of home. Today, White Sonora is sometimes called Kino Wheat after Padre Kino, who was one of the more well-known Jesuit missionaries of the American Southwest in the 1600s.

This exchange of new foods and crops from East to West and West to East came to be known on a larger scale as the Columbian Exchange. Despite their colonial origins, we see these imported additions folded into the food culture of the Sonoran people over time. At the time of its arrival, soft white wheat competed with corn for the place of pre-eminence at the table, but wheat soon found its place. As White Sonora Wheat was acculturated by the northern Mexicans and later the Akimel O'odham, it found iteration as distinctly Sonoran food – flour tortillas and pinole (a highly nutritious flour-based drink). Today, you can still find cultural imagery throughout the north of Mexico that holds this adopted immigrant wheat up as a point of national pride.

FLAVOR PROFILE

Freshly milled White Sonora is light and creamy with a sweet desert essence.

SUBSTITUTES

Look for heritage soft white wheats with names like Wit Wolkorning and Chiddam Blanc de Mars, or use conventional soft white wheat.

Creamy Buttermilk Salad
WITH QUICK-PICKLED VEGETABLES

Chilled tangy buttermilk dressing is my answer to Phoenix summers, and this salad is guaranteed to refresh, especially if you're lucky enough to enjoy it poolside. There are two tricks to this recipe: the first is to cook the White Sonora berries long enough so that they expand into spheres like large Israeli couscous; the second is to chill the salad in the fridge a few hours to give the flavors time to meld. You'll want to make the pickles ahead of time.

Serves 8 as a side

200 g (7 oz/1 cup) White Sonora Wheat Berries

handful of toasted hazelnuts, crushed

QUICK PICKLES

5 radishes, finely sliced into rounds

1 medium cucumber, sliced lengthwise into thin ribbons

1 fennel bulb, finely sliced

120 ml (4 fl oz/½ cup) white-wine vinegar or apple-cider vinegar

50 g (1¾ oz/¼ cup) granulated sugar

1 tablespoon fine sea salt

HERBY BUTTERMILK DRESSING

120 ml (4 fl oz/½ cup) buttermilk

1 tablespoon white-wine vinegar or apple-cider vinegar

2 tablespoons olive oil

1 garlic clove, finely chopped

small handful of finely chopped chives

small handful of finely chopped dill

1 teaspoon chopped marjoram or thyme (optional)

1 teaspoon chopped tarragon (optional)

1 teaspoon fine sea salt

To make the quick pickles, place the sliced vegetables in a large mason jar, then cover with the vinegar, sugar, salt and 240 ml (8 fl oz/1 cup) water. Secure the lid and shake vigorously to combine, then place the jar in the fridge. These can be prepared up to 3 days ahead. Let them pickle for at least 30 minutes if making them on the same day.

Place the White Sonora berries in a large saucepan, along with 960 ml (32½ fl oz/4 cups) water, and simmer over a medium heat for 40–60 minutes until the berries expand into small spheres like large Israeli couscous. Drain and leave to cool completely. If you cook the berries ahead of time, store them in their cooking liquid in the fridge for up to a week.

To make the dressing, mix together all the ingredients in a large bowl.

To assemble the salad, drain the quick pickles and add to the bowl, along with the cold White Sonora berries and hazelnuts. Toss to combine, then chill well before serving.

Cauliflower & Date
White Sonora Berry Salad
WITH CREAMY WALNUT AND CAPER PESTO

This is a departure from my usual grain salad formula (wheat berry, fruit, cheese, nuts and vinaigrette), where the wheat berries generally take the place of greens. In this dish, they stand in for pasta, echoing an Israeli couscous salad, with the coarse pesto adding texture and a punchy flavor. This versatile salad can be served either warm or chilled.

Serves 8 as a side

200 g (7 oz/1 cup) White Sonora Wheat Berries

1 head cauliflower, cut into bite-sized florets

3 dates, pitted and roughly chopped

1 tablespoon olive oil

½ teaspoon fine sea salt

Italian (flat-leaf) parsley leaves, to garnish (optional)

WALNUT AND CAPER PESTO

130 g (4½ oz/1 cup) walnuts

2 tablespoons olive oil

1 bunch Italian (flat-leaf) parsley, leaves picked and roughly chopped

50 g (1¾ oz/½ cup) grated parmesan

1 tablespoon capers, rinsed if salt-packed

grated zest of 1 lemon

Preheat the oven to 175°C (350°F).

Place the White Sonora berries in a large saucepan, along with 960 ml (32½ fl oz/4 cups) water, and simmer over a medium heat for 40–60 minutes until the berries expand into small spheres like large Israeli couscous. Drain and leave to cool completely. If you cook the berries ahead of time, store them in their cooking liquid in the fridge for up to a week.

Toss together the cauliflower, dates, olive oil and salt in a large bowl. Spread them out evenly on a rimmed baking sheet and roast for 30 minutes, or until the cauliflower is tender when tested with a fork. Set aside to cool slightly (or completely if you prefer a cold salad).

Meanwhile, to make the pesto, place all the ingredients and 120 ml (4 fl oz/½ cup) water in a food processor and pulse to a coarse paste. I like to leave some texture to create a nice mouthfeel in the final dish.

Toss together the cooled wheat berries, roasted cauliflower and date mixture and pesto in a large bowl, garnish with extra parsley, if desired, and serve.

Summer Stone Fruit White Sonora Berry Salad

WITH CANDIED PECANS AND CRISPY PROSCIUTTO

This recipe was created by my mom. While she tries to keep a healthy distance from Dad's and my harebrained ideas, she is always happy to cook with the products we make. She's a genius when it comes to balancing flavors and colors in a dish, and she's famous for her perfectly composed menus at every holiday and family celebration. A few weeks before Christmas, she sends out the master holiday menu to all her children – an entire week of breakfasts, lunches and dinners. We drool. My siblings immediately book their tickets home.

My favorite stone fruit to use in this salad is nectarines, but since a perfectly ripe nectarine can be hard to find, peaches make a great substitute.

Serves 8 as a side

200 g (7 oz/1 cup) White Sonora Wheat Berries

170 g (6 oz) prosciutto, finely sliced (see Tip)

120 g (4½ oz/1 cup) candied pecans (store-bought are fine), coarsely crushed

3 nectarines or other stone fruit, stones removed and sliced

110 g (4 oz) blue cheese, crumbled

2 large handfuls of baby arugula (rocket)

3 mint sprigs, leaves picked and finely chopped

DRESSING

60 ml (2 fl oz/¼ cup) olive oil

2 tablespoons champagne vinegar or white-wine vinegar

1 tablespoon Dijon mustard

1 teaspoon preserved lemon paste (see Tip)

juice of ½ orange

Place the White Sonora berries in a large saucepan along with 960 ml (32½ fl oz/4 cups) water and simmer over a medium heat for 40–60 minutes until the berries expand into small spheres like large Israeli couscous. Drain and leave to cool completely. If you cook the berries ahead of time, store them in their cooking liquid in the fridge for up to a week.

Pan-fry the prosciutto until crispy. Remove and drain on paper towel.

To make the dressing, mix together all the ingredients in a small bowl.

When you are ready to serve, combine the wheat berries, crispy prosciutto, candied pecans, nectarine slices and blue cheese in a large bowl. Add the dressing and toss to coat. Pile the grain salad onto a bed of arugula, finish with a sprinkling of mint and serve.

TIPS

Prosciutto can be difficult to cut. Here's how I do it – stack the slices and roll them up, then slice finely and separate with your hands into long thin pieces.

If you don't have any preserved lemon paste, substitute with the grated zest of 1 lemon and 1 teaspoon fine sea salt.

White Sonora Berry Chili

I sometimes wonder what my teenage self would think of my current enthusiasm for electric pressure cookers. I think they are amazing, and have been known to tout them to unsuspecting strangers at the grocery store; I also teach a whole class on their uses at the mill. A pressure cooker doesn't always cut back on total cooking time, but it does give you a very simple, hands-off, one-pot meal – perfect for busy family life. I think it makes wheat berry recipes less intimidating, so I have included pressure cooker instructions with this recipe and a few others throughout the book for my fellow enthusiasts.

Serves 12

1 tablespoon olive oil

1 large onion, diced

4 garlic cloves, peeled

450 g (1 lb) lean ground beef

2 dried pasilla negro chilies (or ancho chilies), seeds removed, finely chopped

1 tablespoon chili powder

2 teaspoons ground cumin

2 teaspoons smoked paprika

1 teaspoon fine sea salt

1 × 650 g (1 lb 7 oz) jar crushed tomatillos, including the liquid (see Tip)

1 × 800 g (1 lb 12 oz) can diced tomatoes, including the liquid

200 g (7 oz/1 cup) White Sonora Wheat Berries

240 g (8½ oz/1 cup) dried pinto beans (or other similar-sized beans)

240 ml (8 fl oz/1 cup) chicken stock (optional)

GARNISH

1 avocado, sliced

2 tablespoons finely chopped cilantro (coriander)

115 g (4 oz/½ cup) Greek yogurt

lime wedges

Set the pressure cooker to sauté. When it reads 'hot' add the olive oil, onion and garlic to the pot and sauté for 5 minutes, or until the onion is translucent. Add the beef, dried chili, ground spices and salt and cook for 5 minutes, breaking up any large chunks with a wooden spoon as it browns. Add the tomatillos and diced tomatoes and their juices, along with the White Sonora berries and the dried beans.

Close the pressure cooker lid and lock. Set to high pressure for 50 minutes. Make sure the steam valve is closed. Allow the pressure cooker to release naturally (it takes about 30 minutes). When it's ready, the beans should be soft and the wheat berries puffed into chewy balls. If you find the chili is too thick, add some or all of the chicken stock to get it to your preferred consistency.

You can also make this chili on the stove top. Cover and simmer for the same cooking time, giving it an occasional stir until the beans are soft and the wheat berries are puffed and round.

Serve the chili warm topped with sliced avocado, cilantro, a dollop of Greek yogurt and a squeeze of lime.

TIP

If you can't source tomatillos, use salsa verde instead.

Any-Grain Egg Pasta Dough

This is more of a math equation than a recipe. Don't worry, you can use a calculator. The thing is, *every egg has a slightly different weight*, so weighing your ingredients makes it easier to achieve a consistently hydrated dough. If you keep backyard chickens, the variation in size is even more pronounced. For those who don't have access to a scale or simply hate math, I've also given the basic recipe and you can adjust the hydration by feel. This dough is my go-to for a wide range of pasta shapes, including spaghetti, pappardelle, ravioli and cavatelli.

Freshly milled flour is a joy to work with. It's slightly oily, like powdered silk, and it feels pillowy and light between the fingers. I always enjoy a slight sense of drama when I'm working a dough – mixing together a dry shaggy ball, convinced it's not going to work this time, and then right before my eyes, it suddenly transforms into a smooth, elastic mound of perfect dough. Somehow it's a fresh surprise every time; it's really fun!

You could mix your dough in a food processor, but I recommend making it on the counter or a wooden board to get the full sensory experience.

Serves 8

PASTA DOUGH BY RATIO

weigh 3 eggs

divide the weight of the eggs by 0.64; this number will give you the weight of the flour

any flour can be used, but my favorite combination is 65% White Sonora Type 00 and 35% semolina flour

PASTA DOUGH BY MEASURE

160 g (5½ oz/1 cup) White Sonora Type 00 Flour

70 g (2½ oz/heaped ⅓ cup) semolina flour

3 eggs

TIP

You can buy this ratio of Type 00 and semolina pre-mixed as our Hayden Flour Mills Pasta Flour.

Measure out the flour onto the counter or a large wooden board. Use your fingers to form a wide well in the middle of the flour. Crack the eggs into the well and beat the yolks and whites with a fork until combined. Slowly incorporate the flour into the egg mixture while keeping the wall of the well intact (this will keep the egg mixture from running out all over the counter). Continue to work in the flour until the egg is no longer runny. Use a bench scraper to scrape and cut the rest of the flour into the egg until it starts to form a dough.

Use the heel of your hand to vigorously knead the dough for 5 minutes, making sure any dry bits of flour are incorporated. It should be a smooth and elastic ball when you are finished.

If the dough is sticking to your work surface, lightly dust it with 1–2 teaspoons of flour and work it into the dough. Repeat if it continues to stick. Alternatively, if your dough is too dry and doesn't form a cohesive ball, wet your hands and work the moisture into the dough. Repeat if the dough continues to crumble. Make the adjustments in small increments; usually this is all the dough needs.

Cover the dough with an airtight wrap and set aside to rest at room temperature for 30 minutes, or chill in the fridge for 24 hours.

Unwrap the rested dough and cut it into six sections. Work with one section at a time and keep the remaining dough covered so it doesn't dry out. Form the dough into your preferred pasta shape and cook in a pot of well-salted boiling water for 3–5 minutes until al dente.

Crespelle Cannelloni
WITH SAUTÉED CHARD AND GROUND LAMB

Robbie was the chef at Pane Bianco, the restaurant whose back room hosted our very first milling operation. When I got engaged, I begged Robbie to cater my wedding. Once he agreed, I casually mentioned that we had invited three hundred people ... What can I say? We're popular!

I traded middlings (grain scraps for animal feed) from the mill with a local farmer for a lamb, which Robbie slow-cooked to perfection in a Caja China roasting box. I milled 11 kilograms (25 pounds) of White Sonora Wheat and Robbie and his crew made six hundred crespelle. I would feel bad about tricking him into such a Herculean task, except the wedding feast was so delicious that it's impossible to regret it. Assuming you won't be having hundreds of people for dinner, I've reduced the quantities here to serve six to eight lucky guests.

Crespelle are a cross between a crepe and pasta, so they take the place of the noodles in this dish. Filled with seasoned lamb, rolled up and baked in a creamy white sauce, this decadent cannelloni would make a great main for a winter holiday.

Serves 6–8

CRESPELLE

160 g (5½ oz/1 cup) White Sonora Type 00 Flour (see Tip)

3 eggs

240 ml (8 fl oz/1 cup) whole (full-cream) milk

1 teaspoon fine sea salt

1 tablespoon melted butter, cooled to room temperature

WHITE SAUCE

85 g (3 oz/6 tablespoons) butter

40 g (1½ oz/¼ cup) White Sonora Type 00 flour

960 ml (32½ fl oz/4 cups) whole (full-cream) milk

1 teaspoon fine sea salt

50 g (1¾ oz/½ cup) grated parmesan

To make the crespelle, blend all the ingredients in a blender until smooth. Heat a 23 cm (9 in) non-stick frying pan or crepe pan over a medium heat. Pour in 60 ml (2 fl oz/¼ cup) of the batter and tilt the pan to spread it evenly over the base. Cook for 1 minute each side until golden but still soft and pliable, then transfer to a plate. Repeat with the remaining batter to make 12 crepes in all, stacking them up on the plate as you go.

For the white sauce, melt the butter in a medium heavy-based saucepan over a medium heat. Add the flour and mix with a wooden spoon until it is fully incorporated. Pour in the milk, then increase the heat and bring to a boil. Reduce the heat to medium and cook, stirring frequently, for 10 minutes, or until the sauce has thickened enough to coat the back of the spoon. Stir in the salt and parmesan until melted and smooth, then remove from the heat and set aside.

To make the filling, heat the olive oil in a cast-iron skillet or frying pan over a medium heat, add the leek and chard stems and sauté until soft, about 5 minutes. Add the lamb, dried herbs, garlic powder, salt and pepper flakes and cook, stirring regularly and breaking up any large chunks of lamb, for 5–7 minutes until browned and cooked through. Add the chard leaves and cook for another 10 minutes or so until wilted and combined.

Stir half of the white sauce into the lamb mixture, then set aside to cool to room temperature.

LAMB FILLING

1 tablespoon olive oil
2 leeks, finely sliced
1 bunch Swiss chard (silverbeet), leaves and stems separated and finely chopped
450 g (1 lb) ground (minced) lamb (see Tip)
2 tablespoons dried oregano
2 teaspoons dried thyme
¼ teaspoon garlic powder
1 teaspoon fine sea salt
1 teaspoon red pepper flakes

TO FINISH

2 tablespoons finely chopped Italian (flat-leaf) parsley
25 g (1 oz/¼ cup) grated parmesan

Preheat the oven to 230°C (450°F). Have a 30 cm × 23 cm (12 in × 9 in) baking dish ready.

Fill each crespelle with about ½ cup of the filling and roll up to enclose. Place the rolls in a snug single layer in the baking dish, seam-side down, then spoon over the remaining white sauce and sprinkle with the parsley and parmesan. Bake for 20 minutes, or until the cheese begins to brown. Allow the cannelloni to set and cool for 15 minutes before serving.

TIPS

Type 00 can be swapped with einkorn flour (140 g = 5 oz/1 cup). Add an extra 60 ml (2 fl oz/¼ cup) of milk to the batter as the einkorn flour will absorb more liquid.

Replace the ground lamb with ground beef, if preferred.

Pici Pasta

WITH LEMON CREAM SAUCE

Pici is a traditional Tuscan shape. It's like a very thick spaghetti made from a soft dough and it pairs well with creamy sauces. Pici is a great pasta for beginners as it doesn't require any fancy tools – all you need is a rolling pin, a wooden board and your hands. And because there is no egg in this dough, it is very soft and easy to work with. Truly, if you learned how to roll playdough snakes in kindergarten, you should be all set to make this. Once you catch the pasta-making bug in full force, you can start putting all sorts of wild-looking pasta tools on your Christmas list. I certainly do.

The cooking water from handmade pasta is gold. During preparation the pasta is dusted in flour or semolina to keep it from sticking, and this washes off in the boiling water. Make sure you reserve some of this salty, starchy liquid to stir into your final pasta dish; it adds a wonderful creamy consistency as it brings everything together.

Serves 4

320 g (11½ oz/2 cups) White Sonora Type 00 Flour

olive oil, for brushing

semolina flour, for dusting

2 tablespoons basil leaves, to garnish

freshly ground black pepper

LEMON CREAM SAUCE

2 lemons

1 tablespoon olive oil

3 garlic cloves, finely chopped

240 ml (8 fl oz/1 cup) heavy (thick/double) cream

100 g (3½ oz/1 cup) finely grated parmesan (microplaned if possible)

fine sea salt

Place the flour in a large bowl, add 210 ml (7 fl oz) warm water and mix together with a wooden spoon until the flour is hydrated and starts to come together in a shaggy ball. Turn the dough out onto a lightly floured work surface and knead for 5 minutes. If the dough is sticking to your work surface, lightly dust it with 1–2 teaspoons of flour and work it into the dough. Repeat if it continues to stick. Alternatively, if your dough is too dry and doesn't form a cohesive ball, wet your hands and work the moisture into the dough. Repeat if the dough continues to crumble. Make the adjustments in small increments; usually this is all the dough needs.

Cover the dough with an airtight wrap and set aside to rest at room temperature for 30 minutes, or chill in the fridge for 24 hours.

Unwrap the dough and roll it out into a flat round, then fold it in half and roll it flat again. Repeat another five or six times to knead the dough, finishing with a flat disk about 25 cm × 20 cm (10 in × 8 in). Brush the top and side of the dough with olive oil to prevent it from drying out while you work.

Cut the dough into 1 cm (½ in) thick strips. Take one strip and use the palm of your hand to roll the dough into a long thin snake, approximately the same thickness as a phone-charging cord. The noodles will puff up a bit as they cook, so thinner is better.

Once you've rolled them all, dust with semolina flour and leave the noodles to dry for 10 minutes before boiling in a saucepan of salted water for 2–3 minutes.

Meanwhile, start preparing the lemon sauce. Grate the zest of the lemons, then squeeze the juice of one and finely slice the other for garnish. Heat the olive oil in a deep medium frying pan or sauté pan over a medium heat and cook the garlic and lemon zest until fragrant. Add the cream and simmer over a very low heat until heated through.

Drain the pici, reserving about 60 ml (2 fl oz/¼ cup) of the cooking water. Add the pasta and reserved water to the sauce and stir to combine. Gradually add the parmesan and stir until it melts into the creamy sauce. Add the freshly squeezed lemon juice, to taste, and season with salt. Garnish with the basil and sliced lemon, add some fresh pepper to taste, and serve.

WHITE SONORA

White Sonora Celebration Cake

WITH RHUBARB AND PISTACHIO

The classic American white cake is the epitome of industrialized milling methods and the sterilized flours they produce. So I took it as a personal challenge to create a cake that wasn't too rustic, but also wasn't simply a fancy imitation of a nondescript boxed cake. Stone-milled flours tend to absorb more moisture, so the key to preventing a dry crumb is to use coconut oil. It took some time but I finally got the balance right, throwing back to the simple joy of the cakes we grew up on, with just enough sophistication to suit our grown-up palates. This is the perfect cake for any celebration, one that will hopefully become part of your kitchen repertoire and form a nostalgia all of its own.

Serves 8–10

580 g (1 lb 4 oz/3½ cups + 2 tablespoons) White Sonora Type 00 Flour

1½ tablespoons baking powder

1 teaspoon fine sea salt

180 ml (6 fl oz/¾ cup) melted coconut oil or vegetable oil

500 g (1 lb 2 oz/2½ cups) granulated sugar

4 eggs

3 egg yolks

1 tablespoon vanilla extract

350 ml (12 fl oz/1½ cups) whole (full-cream) milk

60 g (2 oz/½ cup) raw pistachio kernels, coarsely ground

RHUBARB BUTTERCREAM

335 g (12 oz) rhubarb (fresh or frozen), chopped

3 egg whites

150 g (5½ oz/¾ cup) granulated sugar

225 g (8 oz/1 cup) unsalted butter, at room temperature, cubed

Preheat the oven to 175°C (350°F). Grease two 23 cm (9 in) round cake pans with vegetable oil and line the base with parchment (baking) paper.

In a medium bowl, whisk together the flour, baking powder and salt. Set aside.

In the bowl of a stand mixer fitted with the paddle attachment, beat the oil and sugar until combined. Add the eggs one at a time, making sure each egg is fully incorporated before adding the next. Add the yolks in the same way, then beat in the vanilla. Gradually add the dry ingredients and the milk in alternating batches and mix to combine. Use a rubber spatula to scrape the side and bottom of the bowl to make sure all the dry ingredients are incorporated, then briefly mix again.

Divide the batter evenly between the prepared cake pans and smooth the surface. Place them on the middle shelf of the oven and bake for 35 minutes, or until golden brown and a skewer inserted in the center comes out clean. Remove and cool in the pans for 10 minutes, then invert the cakes onto wire racks and allow to cool completely.

To make the buttercream, warm the rhubarb in a small saucepan over a low heat for about 15 minutes until it starts to collapse and soften. Stir and mash the rhubarb into a smooth puree, then set aside to cool completely.

Place the egg whites and sugar in the clean bowl of your stand mixer. Bring 480 ml (16 fl oz/2 cups) water to the boil in a small saucepan and place the bowl on top, making sure the base does not touch the water. Gently heat the egg whites and sugar, whisking occasionally, until the sugar has dissolved and the temperature reaches 70°C (160°F). Transfer the bowl to the stand mixer fitted with the whisk attachment and whisk on high speed

TIP
The cooked cakes may be
wrapped and refrigerated for
up to 2 days before frosting,
or frozen for up to a month.
The frosted cake will keep in an
airtight container in the fridge
for up to 3 days.

for 5 minutes, or until stiff, glossy peaks form. Add the butter
one cube at a time while whisking on medium speed. When all
the butter has been incorporated, add the cooled rhubarb puree
and mix on low speed until it's just combined. If the mixture
appears curdled after adding the rhubarb, continue to mix for a
few more minutes until smooth. Store in the fridge if you're not
using the buttercream immediately.

Check your cakes – if they are domed, shave off the top of the
bottom cake layer with a serrated knife to flatten the surface.
Spread one-third of the buttercream over the bottom layer and
sprinkle with half the pistachios. Place the second cake layer on
top and spread the remaining buttercream evenly over the top
and side. Sprinkle over the remaining pistachios and serve.

Pillowy Cinnamon Rolls

All my babies have required cinnamon rolls for proper gestation.
My theory is that cinnamon must provide some key nutrient to
fetal development, so my pregnant body craves it. It's all very scientific,
you see. The cream cheese frosting and fluffy roll are just a convenient
vehicle of cinnamon delivery.

One of the challenges we face with artisan baked goods (like cinnamon
rolls) is that they are held up to their industrially produced counterparts,
and these industrial foods require industrial ingredients. Their flavor,
color and texture is a direct result of roller milling or bleaching. For the
most part, I have weaned myself off these industrial ideals and much prefer
the 'real thing'. Bread, pastries and pastas made from our beautiful grains
are hands down the winner, so I never try to mimic those industrial taste
standards in an attempt to create 'healthy' versions of 'fake' foods.

But I almost came unstuck when I started making cinnamon rolls. I needed
a roll that could also double as a pillow – a great big gooey fluff that would
take me back to the suburban mall of my childhood. Would it be too much
to ask a heritage stone-milled grain to do this for me? IT WOULD NOT.
With the help of instant potato flakes (my secret weapon),
these cinnamon rolls deliver on every level. Bring on the cravings –
they've more than met their match.

Makes 12

8 g (¼ oz/1¼ teaspoons) instant dry yeast

100 g (3½ oz/½ cup) granulated sugar

55 g (2 oz/⅔ cup) instant potato flakes

535 g (1 lb 3 oz /3⅓ cups) White Sonora Type 00 Flour

350 ml (12 fl oz/1½ cups) whole (full-cream) milk, warm

60 ml (2 fl oz/4 tablespoons) melted unsalted butter

1½ teaspoons fine sea salt

2 eggs

Lightly grease a large mixing bowl with butter or oil, ready for proofing the dough. Set aside.

Combine the yeast, granulated sugar and 60 ml (2 fl oz/¼ cup) warm water in the bowl of a stand mixer and stir with a wooden spoon to moisten the yeast and sugar. Add the potato flakes and flour and stir to combine. Add the warm milk, melted butter and salt. Place the bowl on the stand, fit the dough hook and mix on low speed. Add the eggs, one at a time, then continue mixing for 10 minutes, stopping the mixer occasionally to scrape down the side. If the dough is very sticky and not coming away from the side of the bowl, add an additional 1–2 tablespoons flour. Continue mixing for another 7–10 minutes until the dough comes together in a smooth ball.

Turn out the dough onto a generously floured work surface and knead for 5 minutes. Place the dough in the prepared proofing bowl, cover tightly with airtight wrap and place in a warm area of the kitchen for 1½–2 hours until doubled in size. The dough is ready if an indentation remains when touched.

Grease a 33 cm × 23 cm × 5 cm (13 in × 9 in × 2 in) glass or metal baking dish with butter.

Turn the dough out onto a lightly floured work surface and roll it out to a 36 cm × 30 cm (14½ in × 12 in) rectangle.

CINNAMON FILLING

60 g (2 oz/4 tablespoons) unsalted butter

215 g (7½ oz/1 cup) brown sugar

1 tablespoon ground cinnamon

CREAM CHEESE FROSTING

115 g (4 oz/½ cup) unsalted butter, at room temperature

115 g (4 oz) cream cheese, at room temperature

1 teaspoon vanilla extract

pinch of fine sea salt

115 g (4 oz/1 cup) powdered (icing) sugar

For the cinnamon filling, melt the butter, and combine the brown sugar and cinnamon in a small bowl. Brush the surface of the dough with the melted butter, then sprinkle evenly with the cinnamon sugar. Starting at a short end, firmly roll up the dough, pinching the seam to keep the roll tightly sealed. With the seam side down, use a piece of butcher's twine or unflavored dental floss to cut the roll into 12 equal slices by slipping the twine or floss under the roll and crossing the two ends over the top to create a clean slice. Place the slices, spiral-side up, in the prepared baking dish. Cover tightly and proof in a warm area of the kitchen for 30–45 minutes, or until doubled in volume.

Meanwhile, preheat the oven to 190°C (375°F).

Place the dish in the oven and bake until the tops of the rolls are golden brown, about 30–35 minutes. Remove and allow to cool completely.

To make the frosting, whisk together the butter and cream cheese in a large bowl until thick and smooth. Mix in the vanilla and salt. Add half the powdered sugar and whisk for about 30 seconds until smooth, then repeat with the remaining sugar.

Spread the frosting over the cooled cinnamon rolls and serve.

TIPS

The cinnamon rolls may be baked and cooled, then frozen unfrosted for up to 2 months.

If you want to make a start the night before, prepare the rolls and leave them to proof in the fridge overnight. In the morning, take the dish out of the fridge and bring the rolls to room temperature while the oven preheats, then bake for 30 minutes.

HERITAGE BREAD WHEAT

Becoming a collector of any kind has its pitfalls. The curio cabinets slowly, inevitably, take over your living room and the search for the rarest never-before-seen edition consumes you. We were no exception to the rule when we became heritage grain collectors. However, as much as we'd love to grow and sell every obscure variety of grain known to man, there are practical limitations to what we can stock at the mill, and too many unfamiliar choices can become confusing to customers. So, we typically opt for one variety per grain category that is the most well-loved by chefs and customers. When it came to bread wheats, there were so many beautiful varieties in our collection we couldn't help ourselves – we've made an exception and allowed ourselves two: Red Fife and Rouge de Bordeaux.

When we started the mill, Red Fife was already well into its revival in Canada, where it had been the most popular type of wheat in the nineteenth century before it became all but extinct by the twenty-first century. Just as White Sonora was making a heritage comeback in the Southwest, Canadian farmers had been working to bring back Red Fife as it was one of the first wheats to make its way from Europe in the pockets of Scottish immigrants. This recent revival made it relatively easy to obtain seed.

When we found Rouge de Bordeaux wheat, we knew we had to add it to our offerings. It was a favorite of French bakers in the nineteenth century, and we had to indulge our curiosity about what modern-day bakers would create with this well-storied, traditional varietal. Named for its region of origin in France, ripe Rouge de Bordeaux wheat has a rich, nutty aroma and is high in protein, making it an excellent option for bread baking.

FLAVOR PROFILE

Heritage bread wheats are deeply nutty with strong notes of cinnamon, cacao and brown sugar.

SUBSTITUTES

Look for heritage bread wheats with names like Red Fife, Turkey Red, Rouge de Bordeaux, Marquis, Quanah, Federation Wheat, Red Zanzibar, or use a conventional hard red wheat.

Orange & Anise Knots

WITH ORANGE GLAZE

These charming knots can beautifully round out a brunch menu, see you through an afternoon energy slump, or stand alone as a memorable dessert. While anise can be a somewhat polarizing flavor, the earthy licorice element works well here as it highlights the bright, juicy citrus character of the orange glaze. I first came across this flavor combination when I was developing a more versatile iteration of Spanish olive oil tortas, and I love it just as much in this context.

Weekend project alert! This is one of the more labor-intensive recipes in the book, so make plans to share them with friends who will be suitably impressed by your extraordinary baking talents.

Makes 12

115 g (4 oz/½ cup) unsalted butter

240 ml (8 fl oz/1 cup) whole (full-cream) milk

560 g (1 lb 4 oz/3½ cups) Heritage Bread Flour

2 tablespoons instant dry yeast

100 g (3½ oz/½ cup) granulated sugar

2 teaspoons kosher salt

1 tablespoon anise seeds, finely ground

grated zest of 1 large orange (reserve the juice for the glaze)

2 eggs, lightly beaten

2 teaspoons vanilla extract

FILLING

65 g (2¼ oz/⅓ cup) granulated sugar

70 g (2½ oz/⅓ cup) brown sugar

60 ml (2 fl oz/4 tablespoons) melted unsalted butter

Grease a large mixing bowl with butter or oil, ready for proofing the dough, and a 12-hole regular muffin pan. Set aside.

Combine the butter and milk in a medium microwave-safe bowl and microwave on high for 30 seconds. Check the mixture, then return the bowl to the microwave and continue heating in 10-second intervals until the butter has melted. Set aside.

In the bowl of a stand mixer fitted with the dough hook, combine the flour, yeast, sugar, salt, ground anise and orange zest. Add the warm (but not hot) butter and milk mixture and mix on low speed to combine. Add the egg and vanilla and continue mixing on low speed for another 5 minutes. Remove the bowl from the mixer and use a rubber spatula to scrape the side and base of the bowl to loosen any bits of flour that didn't mix in. Return to the mixer with the dough hook and continue kneading on low speed for another 10 minutes. The dough should cling to the dough hook and feel smooth to the touch.

Turn out the dough onto a lightly floured work surface and knead for 5 minutes, then place in the prepared mixing bowl and flip the dough so it is coated with oil on both sides. Tightly cover the bowl with airtight wrap and leave to proof in a warm spot in the kitchen for 1–1½ hours until doubled in size and the dough springs back when poked.

To prepare the filling, combine the two sugars in a small bowl.

Gently punch down the dough and turn it out onto a lightly floured work surface. With a rolling pin, roll out the dough to a 46 cm × 30 cm (18 in × 12 in) rectangle. Brush the surface with the melted butter, then sprinkle the combined sugars evenly over the top.

Starting at the long side closest to you, fold the bottom third of the dough up and the top third down – as if you were folding a letter. Use the rolling pin to lightly flatten the dough, then cut it crosswise into 12 even strips. Working with one strip at a

GLAZE

3 tablespoons fresh orange juice
(top up with water, if needed)

260 g (9 oz/2¼ cups) powdered
(icing) sugar, sifted

time, use a pastry roller to cut the dough into three equal strips while keeping the top intact. It will look like a three-pronged comb. Braid the three strands together and pinch at the bottom to seal. Roll the braid up towards the uncut end, then place in one of the prepared muffin holes, knot side up. Repeat with the remaining pieces of dough. Tightly cover the pan with airtight wrap and leave to proof in a warm spot for 20 minutes.

Preheat the oven to 175°C (350°F).

Remove the wrap, place the pan in the center of the oven and bake for 20–25 minutes until the knots are golden brown on top, rotating the pan after 10 minutes. Remove from the oven and allow to cool completely.

To prepare the glaze, whisk together the orange juice and the powdered sugar in a medium bowl, adding a little water if you need to thin it down slightly.

Spread an even layer of glaze over the cooled buns and serve. These are best eaten on the day of baking.

See step-by-step images on pages 72–73.

HERITAGE BREAD WHEAT

Za'atar Cracker Sticks

When my husband was a monk in training (see page 11 intro section), he was assigned to live in Beirut, Lebanon, for a few years. Years later, after we were married, we went together for a visit. As well as introducing me to all his friends, he was excited for me to try his favorite food – man'oushe za'atar, warm flatbread cooked on a convex skillet and sprinkled with za'atar and olive oil. Here, I've turned this food memory into crunchy cracker sticks.

This recipe uses the dough from the butter crust skillet pizza on page 76. I'll often make a double batch so I have a quick appetizer on hand for pizza night.

Makes about 30

1 quantity pizza dough (page 76)

2 tablespoons olive oil

3–4 tablespoons za'atar (see Tip)

1 teaspoon flaky sea salt

Preheat the oven to 220°C (425°F). Line two sheet pans (baking sheets) with parchment (baking) paper.

Make the pizza dough and proof until it has doubled in size, then roll it out to a 38 cm (15 in) square. Rub the olive oil over the dough and sprinkle evenly and generously with the za'atar and salt. Cut the dough in half and then slice lengthwise into 2.5 cm (1 in) thick strips. Twist and gently stretch the strips of dough until they are about 20 cm (8 in) long, then place them on the prepared sheet pans, well spaced so they cook evenly.

Bake for 10 minutes, or until golden. Remove and set aside – they will crisp up as they cool. These are most delicious on the day of baking but leftovers will store in an airtight container for up to a week.

TIP

Za'atar is a delicious blend of sesame seeds, thyme, coriander, sumac, Aleppo pepper and salt. You can blend up your own mix, but I usually keep a jar in my pantry. Whatever you use, make sure it's as fresh and fragrant as possible.

Grape Focaccia

Having a phone conversation with my dad is like calling Google, which has earned him the honorary title, 'Google Dad'. It's not because he knows everything off the top of his head; it's because he will literally find the answer to every question ... on Google. He loves researching: before the invention of the internet, the library was his favorite hangout. I often phone him, seeking his hard-earned knowledge on bread baking or pizza dough, and instead of receiving a pearl of timeless wisdom, I hear keys clicking in the background. This recipe is a case in point. I asked if I could include his tried-and-true focaccia in my cookbook, and what did he do? He researched focaccia bread and gave me this one instead. At least his obsession yields delicious results and includes some element of tradition, even if it's not from our family. Adding grapes to focaccia is an Italian harvest custom.

Serves 6

1 medium baking potato, skin on

1½ teaspoons instant dry yeast

185 g (6½ oz/1 heaped cup) Heritage Bread Flour (see Tip)

180 g (6½ oz/1½ cups) all-purpose (plain) flour

1¾ teaspoons fine sea salt

120 ml (4 fl oz/½ cup) olive oil

300 g (10½ oz/1½ cups) Concord or black grapes (see Tip)

2 teaspoons rosemary leaves

Lightly oil a large mixing bowl and set aside.

Place the potato in a small saucepan and cover with water. Bring to a boil and cook for about 25 minutes until the potato is tender and can be easily pierced with a fork. Drain and allow to cool, then peel and grate. Measure out 1½ cups lightly packed potato.

In the bowl of a stand mixer fitted with the dough hook, combine the potato, yeast, flours, salt, 2 tablespoons olive oil and 240 ml (8 fl oz/1 cup) water. Mix for about 5 minutes until it comes together to form a sticky dough. Lightly flour your hands before transferring the dough to the oiled bowl. Cover and leave to proof for 1 hour, or until it has doubled in size.

Oil the bottom of a 46 cm × 33 cm (18 in × 13 in) sheet pan (baking sheet) with 60 ml (2 fl oz/¼ cup) of the remaining olive oil (see Tip).

Pat and stretch the dough to fit the size of the pan, then spread the grapes evenly over the top, lightly pressing them into the dough. Cover loosely with oiled airtight wrap or parchment (baking) paper and leave to rise for about 30 minutes.

Preheat the oven to 220°C (425°F). Uncover the dough, drizzle over the remaining olive oil and sprinkle with the rosemary. Bake for 25 minutes until puffed and golden. Allow to cool completely, cut into squares and serve.

TIPS

If preferred, you can replace the flours in the recipe with 365 g (13 oz/2⅓ cups) of our Artisan Bread Flour.

For a thicker focaccia, use a quarter sheet pan/baking sheet (33 cm × 23 cm/13 in × 9 in). Just give it an extra 5 minutes in the oven.

Blueberries also work beautifully.

Butter Crust Skillet Pizza

WITH FIG JAM AND PROSCIUTTO

If you were an elementary school kid in the '90s, you may, like me, have participated in the semi-renowned 'Book-It!' program, in which young children were bribed into reading a prescribed number of books. The highly motivational prize was not in fact the betterment of our young minds; it was a personal pan pizza from Pizza Hut. Can you imagine a greater incentive? These days I love reading for its own sake and we make our own homemade pizzas as a family. But the nostalgia is strong for a deep-dish, buttery crust pizza that I don't have to share with anyone else.

Baking a pizza in a cast-iron skillet is a great way to get a crispy crust at home without investing in serious pizza-making tools like a stone, peel or a wood-fired oven.

Makes 2 small or 1 large pizza

160 g (5½ oz/1 cup) Heritage Bread Flour

95 g (3¼ oz/½ cup) semolina flour

½ teaspoon fine sea salt

½ teaspoon instant dry yeast

2 tablespoons olive oil

60 ml (2 fl oz/4 tablespoons) melted butter

TOPPING

170 g (6 oz/½ cup) fig jam

pinch of red pepper flakes

85 g (3 oz) prosciutto, roughly torn into large pieces

½ red onion, finely sliced

225 g (8 oz) mozzarella, thickly sliced

1 bunch arugula (rocket)

1 tablespoon olive oil

1 tablespoon red-wine vinegar

Combine the flours, salt, yeast, olive oil and 160 ml (5½ fl oz/⅔ cup) warm water in a large bowl and mix together to form a shaggy ball. Turn out the dough onto a lightly floured work surface and knead for 5 minutes until smooth and elastic. Alternatively, place the ingredients in the bowl of a stand mixer fitted with the dough hook and mix on low speed for 5 minutes.

Shape the dough into a ball, place in a large bowl and cover with a tea towel. Proof for 1–2 hours at room temperature (or up to 18 hours in the fridge) until the dough has doubled in size.

Preheat the oven to 245°C (475°F). If you are making two small pizzas, divide the dough in half and shape into two smooth balls.

Pour the melted butter in the bottom of the skillet, or divide between two smaller pans. Place the dough in the center and use your fingers to flatten it outwards, shaping it into an even round.

Now for the topping. Spread the fig jam evenly over the dough and sprinkle with the red pepper. Top with slices of prosciutto and red onion and cover with mozzarella.

Bake the smaller pizzas for 15 minutes or the large one for 25 minutes. Remove and rest for 5 minutes, then remove from the pan. Toss together the arugula, olive oil and vinegar and scatter over the pizza, then slice and serve.

Blueberry Muffins

WITH TURMERIC AND CINNAMON STREUSEL

A friend remarked that I should rename these 'geode muffins' because, while they are plain-looking on the outside, once broken open they reveal a rusty orange interior studded with blueberry 'gems'. Double batch and freeze for a quick breakfast.

Makes 12

280 g (10 oz/1¾ cups) Heritage Bread Flour

½ tablespoon baking powder

1 teaspoon baking soda (bicarbonate of soda)

1 tablespoon ground turmeric

½ teaspoon ground cinnamon

¼ teaspoon freshly grated nutmeg

¼ teaspoon fine sea salt

115 g (4 oz/½ cup) unsalted butter, at room temperature

100 g (3½ oz/1 cup) granulated sugar

grated zest of ½ lemon

2 eggs

230 g (8 oz/1 cup) Greek yogurt

240 g (8½ oz/1½ cups) fresh or frozen blueberries

CINNAMON STREUSEL

160 g (5½ oz/1 cup) Heritage Bread Flour

110 g (4 oz/½ cup) brown sugar

100 g (3½ oz/½ cup) granulated sugar

1 teaspoon ground cinnamon

¼ teaspoon kosher salt

115 g (4 oz/½ cup) unsalted butter, diced and chilled

To make the streusel, combine the flour, sugars, cinnamon and salt in a large bowl. Add the butter and rub in with your fingertips to create a coarse, crumbly mixture. Don't overwork the butter – some small lumps should still be visible. Use immediately or tip into a container and store in the fridge until needed.

Preheat the oven to 190°C (375°F). Spray a 12-hole regular muffin pan with non-stick baking spray or line with paper cases.

In a medium bowl, whisk together the flour, baking powder, baking soda, turmeric, cinnamon, nutmeg and salt. Set aside.

Place the butter, sugar and lemon zest in the bowl of a stand mixer fitted with the paddle attachment and mix until pale and fluffy. Add the eggs one at a time and mix until fully incorporated. Gradually mix in the flour mixture, then remove the bowl from the stand and stir in the yogurt. Use a spatula to scrape the base and side of the bowl to ensure that everything is well mixed. Gently fold in the blueberries.

Divide the batter evenly between the muffin cups. Generously sprinkle the streusel mixture over the top. Bake for 25 minutes, or until golden brown and a toothpick inserted in the center of a muffin comes out clean.

Allow the muffins to cool in the pan for 10 minutes, then remove and serve. Store any leftovers in an airtight container for up to 2 days. Gently warm through before serving.

Burnstown Date Squares

These date squares will make you friends. At least, that's how it worked for my friend Lucie. She passed around a tin of her mom's date squares at my very first McGill graduate seminar and I decided then and there that this girl would be my new BFF. Luckily for me, she turned out to be smart, funny and loyal, on top of having great taste in baked goods. Our blossoming friendship was enriched by more shared tins of sweets from her mom, along with a complete Canadian education – from ice fishing and maple tapping to canal skating and poutine eating.

I discovered that date squares are a classic Canadian potluck staple, so it makes sense to give them an update with Canada's own heritage wheat, Red Fife. This recipe is named after the utterly charming village on the Ottawa River where Lucie grew up: Burnstown, Ontario.

Makes 16

160 g (5½ oz/1 cup) Red Fife or Heritage Bread Flour

120 g (4½ oz/1 cup) oat flour (see page 48)

½ teaspoon baking soda (bicarbonate of soda)

¼ teaspoon fine sea salt

½ teaspoon ground cinnamon

½ teaspoon ground cardamom

225 g (8 oz/1 cup) butter, diced and chilled

215 g (7½ oz/1 cup) brown sugar

DATE FILLING

340 g (12 oz) pitted dates

grated zest of 1 lemon

1 teaspoon vanilla extract

Preheat the oven to 165°C (325°F) and line a 20 cm (8 in) square cake pan with parchment (baking) paper.

To make the date filling, place the dates in a small saucepan, add 240 ml (8 fl oz/1 cup) water and simmer over a medium heat for about 5 minutes until the dates have softened. Remove the pan from the heat and mash with a wooden spoon into a smooth paste. Stir in the lemon zest and vanilla, then set aside.

Place the flours, baking soda, salt and ground spices in a food processor, add the butter and pulse until the mixture resembles coarse cornmeal. Pulse in the brown sugar until evenly distributed.

Firmly press two-thirds of the dough into the base of the prepared pan. Add the date filling, smoothing it out evenly with a spatula, then lightly sprinkle over the remaining crumbly dough. Bake for 30–40 minutes until the top is golden and the date filling is bubbling through the crumble.

Remove and allow to cool completely in the pan. Use a sharp knife to cut into 16 squares and serve. Leftovers will keep in an airtight container at room temperature or in the fridge for up to a week.

Classic Honey Graham Crackers

WITH CINNAMON SUGAR

After a good rainfall, our Red Fife wheat field gives off strong aromas similar to cinnamon and cocoa. In time, I was able to tell when Red Fife was running through the mill by the trademark graham cracker smell wafting into the warehouse. Obviously this flour is begging to be made into a simple graham cracker, where its cinnamon notes can shine. Around the holidays, I swap out the honey for molasses and add a dash of ground ginger and grated orange zest for a darker, wintry cookie.

Makes about 24

240 g (8½ oz/1½ cups) Red Fife or Heritage Bread Flour

¼ teaspoon ground cinnamon

170 g (6 oz/¾ cup) unsalted butter, at room temperature

110 g (4 oz/½ cup) brown sugar

½ teaspoon fine sea salt

2 tablespoons honey

turbinado or raw sugar, for sprinkling

Combine the flour and cinnamon in a small bowl and set aside.

Place the butter, brown sugar, salt and honey in the bowl of a stand mixer fitted with the paddle attachment and mix until completely incorporated. Add the cinnamon flour and mix until a dough starts to form.

Turn out the dough onto a work surface and gently press it into a ball, being careful not to overwork it. Flatten it into a disc, then wrap in airtight wrap and rest in the fridge for at least 30 minutes.

Preheat the oven to 175°C (350°F). Line two cookie sheets with parchment (baking) paper.

On a lightly floured work surface, roll out the dough to a 5–6 mm (¼ in) thickness, then cut into 7.5 cm × 5 cm (3 in × 2 in) rectangles (or other shape if preferred; you can use a fluted or scalloped-edge cookie cutter, for instance). Transfer the cookies to the prepared sheets and prick the surface with a fork, then sprinkle with turbinado or raw sugar.

Bake for 8–10 minutes until dry in appearance and deliciously fragrant. Remove and allow to cool completely. Store in an airtight container at room temperature for up to a week.

FARRO

A hallmark trait of ancient and heritage grains is their tall stature. In contrast to modern wheats that typically only grow to about calf height, heritage grains will grow to my waist and sometimes over my head. A good rule of thumb in farming is that what we see above ground is mirrored underground; the taller the wheat is, the deeper the roots go. A plant with deep roots is amazing in its ability to pull up micronutrients from the soil and prevent topsoil erosion. Farro is a prime example of these tall and impressive grains.

Farro also has a deep history to match its roots – a 10,000-year history to be precise. Originating from the Fertile Crescent (what we know as modern-day Iran, Iraq, Jordan, Syria and Palestine), farro is what the pharaohs ate. It's the grain that Jesus and his disciples ate to satisfy their hunger as they walked through the wheat fields on the Sabbath.

We would still be subsisting on farro today if it weren't for one pesky trait of this ancient grain: its hull. Each grain of farro is encased in a tough outer shell. This inedible shell has to be removed before the grain can be eaten or milled. We have specialized equipment that peels this outer husk off and frees the grain, but I often wonder how this gnarly task was done pre-mechanization. And I am not the only one; there are archives of scientific articles specifically devoted to speculation on how ancient peoples might have removed the outer hull. This trait was slowly selected against until we had free-threshing wheats, where the grain would easily fall from the wheat head, ready to be cooked or milled.

FLAVOR PROFILE

Farro resembles a plumper wild brown rice and tastes of toasted walnuts with light caramelly notes.

SUBSTITUTES

You will sometimes see farro referred to as Emmer Farro. This helps distinguish it from a few other types of grain that farro is used for in the Italian languages. If you can't find farro berries or farro flour, spelt or Khorasan (sometimes sold as Kamut) make a good substitute.

Pickled Cherry Farro Salad

WITH KALE AND GOAT'S CHEESE

The love of pickles runs deep in my family: homemade pickles,
giant gas-station pickles, pickles on popcorn, pickle-juice cocktails,
fried pickles, pickles straight out of the jar for an after-school snack ...
It's understandable, then, that pickling features in many of our grain
salads, as they always benefit from a vinegary hit.

My foolproof combo for grain salads is this: a cooked whole grain,
pickled vegetables or fruit, cheese, nuts, something green and a bit of
salt and pepper. Within those parameters the combinations are endless.
This one is a favorite. If I'm serving it near Christmas, I swap out the
pickled cherries for cranberries, giving it a welcome festive flourish.

Serves 8

190 g (6½ oz/1 cup) Farro Berries

60 ml (2 fl oz/¼ cup) olive oil

1 bunch Tuscan (Lacinato) kale
or cavolo nero, stems removed,
leaves cut into bite-sized pieces

225 g (8 oz) goat's cheese,
crumbled

85 g (3 oz/¾ cup) pecans,
roughly chopped

fine sea salt

freshly ground black pepper

PICKLED CHERRIES

280 g (10 oz/2 cups) fresh
cherries, pitted

60 ml (2 fl oz/¼ cup) balsamic
vinegar

50 g (1¾ oz/¼ cup) granulated
sugar

1 cinnamon stick

2 teaspoons black peppercorns

To make the pickled cherries, place the cherries in a medium
mason jar. Bring the vinegar, sugar, cinnamon stick,
peppercorns and 240 ml (8 fl oz/1 cup) water to a boil in a small
saucepan, then reduce the heat and simmer for 5 minutes until
the sugar has dissolved. Pour the hot pickling liquid over the
cherries. Cool to room temperature, then cover and refrigerate
for at least 6 hours and up to 3 weeks.

Place the farro berries in a medium saucepan and pour in
enough water to cover by 7.5 cm (3 in). Bring to a boil, then
reduce the heat and simmer for 40 minutes, or until the berries
have softened but are still chewy. Set aside to cool. Drain the
berries to remove any excess water.

Using your hands, gently massage the kale – it will start to wilt,
making the leaves less stiff and rubbery.

Toss together the cooled farro, olive oil, kale, goat's cheese,
pecans and pickled cherries in a serving bowl, season to taste
with salt and pepper and serve.

Chocolate-Flecked Farro Banana Bread

It's a bit like choosing a favorite child, but if you really twisted my arm I would admit that farro is my favorite grain. Besides having the flavor of toasted walnuts, it has the seniority of being among the world's oldest grains. There are very few recipes for farro flour, so I began by using it in place of half the flour in my favorite baked goods. Recently I tried replacing the whole lot with farro flour and found to my delight that it always works! There's no turning back now.

This is a very basic banana bread recipe, designed to let the farro flour shine and convince you of the ease and deliciousness of heritage grain swaps in your baking. This is a perfect recipe to bookmark if you're just getting started, or are perhaps a bit skeptical about baking with these new flours.

Serves 8

3 ripe bananas (see Tip)

115 g (4 oz/½ cup) Greek yogurt

1 teaspoon vanilla extract

60 ml (2 fl oz/¼ cup) melted coconut oil

110 g (4 oz/½ cup) brown sugar

2 eggs

200 g (7 oz/1¼ cups) Farro Flour

1 teaspoon baking soda (bicarbonate of soda)

¼ teaspoon fine sea salt

½ teaspoon ground cinnamon

¼ teaspoon freshly grated nutmeg (optional)

60 g (2 oz) bittersweet dark chocolate

2 tablespoons turbinado or raw sugar

Preheat the oven to 175°C (350°F). Grease or line a 23 cm × 13 cm (9 in × 5 in) loaf (bar) pan with parchment (baking) paper, leaving a 5 cm (2 in) overhang on each long side to help lift the bread out easily.

Mash the bananas in a bowl and mix in the yogurt and vanilla.

In the bowl of a stand mixer fitted with the paddle attachment, beat the coconut oil and brown sugar together on medium speed, adding the eggs one at a time. Mix for about 3 minutes until creamy and light in color, then add the banana mixture and mix on low speed until combined.

In a separate bowl, whisk together the flour, baking soda, salt, cinnamon and nutmeg. Slowly add to the banana batter and mix on low speed until just combined.

Using a sharp knife, splinter the chocolate. This doesn't have to be a precise process as varying sizes of chocolate will create the flecked look when you slice into the banana bread. Gently fold the chocolate into the batter – be careful not to overmix or let the chocolate melt into the mixture.

Pour the batter into the prepared pan and smooth the surface, then sprinkle the turbinado or raw sugar evenly over the top. Bake for 50 minutes, or until a skewer inserted into the center comes out clean. Cool in the pan for 10 minutes, then turn out onto a rack to cool completely. Cut into thick slices. Leftovers will keep in an airtight container for up to 4 days.

TIP

I always have a stash of very ripe black bananas in the freezer. I set the bananas on the counter in a bowl to thaw for an hour or two before I start baking. Interestingly, I've found that letting the ripe bananas sit out for longer, say the whole day, gives them a nice caramelized flavor.

FARRO

Farro Coconut Pudding

I am always reminding our grains and flours that they can be anything they want to be when they grow up. And it's true; there's really nothing these heritage grains can't do. I know this because I keep putting them to the test. Rice pudding is my favorite dessert of all time, and at first I was skeptical about whether farro could successfully replace the rice, but it turns out that farro is a worthy competitor. Is it better than the original rice version? I'll let you decide.

Serves 6–8

190 g (6½ oz/1 cup) Farro Berries

1.1 liters (36½ fl oz/4½ cups) whole (full-cream) milk

100 g (3½ oz/½ cup) granulated sugar

1 cinnamon stick

30 g (1 oz/½ cup) unsweetened coconut flakes

1 teaspoon fine sea salt

1 egg, lightly beaten with 120 ml (4 fl oz/½ cup) whole (full-cream) milk

1 tablespoon vanilla extract

15 g (½ oz/1 tablespoon) unsalted butter

230 g (8 oz/1 cup) heavy (thick/double) cream

your choice of fresh fruit or toasted coconut, to garnish (optional)

Place the farro berries in a medium saucepan and pour in enough water to cover by 7.5 cm (3 in). Bring to a boil, then reduce the heat and simmer for 40 minutes, or until the berries have softened but are still chewy. Set aside to cool.

Drain the berries to remove any excess water, then measure out 160 g (5½ oz/1 cup) and set aside.

Return the remaining farro to the pan you cooked it in, add the milk and blend with a stick blender to a puree – it won't be perfectly smooth. (You could also use a food processor or upright blender to do this.) Stir in the reserved cup of farro, along with the sugar, cinnamon stick, coconut and salt.

Bring the mixture to a simmer over a medium heat, stirring often to prevent scorching. Run your finger down the back of your wooden spoon; if it leaves a trail, it's reached the right consistency. If not, cook for another couple of minutes and test again.

Using a whisk, quickly stir in the egg and milk mixture and cook for about 5 minutes until the pudding returns to a slow simmer and begins to bubble. Remove from the heat and stir in the vanilla and butter until melted and combined. Scoop the pudding into a stainless-steel bowl or shallow baking pan and allow to cool completely, stirring occasionally. Place the pudding in the fridge to chill and set for 2–4 hours or overnight.

Just before serving, whip the cream to soft peaks and fold into the cold pudding. Divide among dessert bowls and garnish with fresh fruit or toasted coconut, if desired.

Crispy Farro Furikake

Growing up, we had a Japanese neighbor who became like an adopted grandma to me and my siblings. She walked so many plates of delicious Japanese food across the street to us kids, and became such a big part of our lives, that we went to a Japanese Saturday school throughout elementary school and took Japanese language classes all the way into high school. Thanks to Michi, inari sushi and korokke are just as much a nostalgic flavor of our childhood as other less sophisticated '80s classics, such as Capri Sun and Oreos.

Furikake is a classic Japanese condiment: sort of like savory sprinkles, packed with umami and laced with a delicate, salty flourish. We kids loved it and put it on everything we ate. It's still a family favorite.

This is more of a technique than a recipe. This process of frying grains can be done with pretty much any cooked grain, such as einkorn, White Sonora, rye and other soft wheats, as well as oat groats. They make crunchy additions to rice bowls, creamy soups, steamed vegetables, salads or the simple perfection of avocado toast.

Makes approx. 330 g (11 oz/ 2 cups)

320 g (11 oz/2 cups) cooked Farro Berries (see Tip)

canola oil, for deep-frying

1 teaspoon soy sauce

½ teaspoon fish sauce

1 tablespoon sesame seeds

5 g (¼ oz) toasted nori, crushed

Drain the cooked grains and spread them out on a tray lined with paper towel to dry while you heat the oil.

Fill a large deep heavy-based saucepan or Dutch oven with 2.5 cm (1 in) oil and heat to 190°C (375°F), or until a cube of bread/couple of farro berries dropped in the oil brown in 15 seconds. Carefully add the cooked farro and deep-fry for 6 minutes, or until it begins to snap and crackle loudly; when it's ready it will turn a dark brown color and start to clump together. Use a mesh ladle to remove the grains and allow to drain and cool on paper towel. They will be crispy with a slight chew but not hard.

Toss the cooled farro with the soy sauce, fish sauce, sesame seeds and nori. Use it straight away, or store in an airtight container in the freezer for up to 3 months.

See image on page 111.

TIP

You'll need about 125 g (4½ oz/⅔ cup) uncooked Farro Berries to make this quantity. Follow the cooking instructions on page 87.

Farmer's Porridge

Farro is a vitreous grain (meaning it's glass-like) so when we stone-mill it, it shatters and we end up with three products: farro semolina, farro flour and farro bran. The farro semolina is the glassy shards of the farro, resembling turbinado sugar; it's such a niche product that it doesn't come up in many recipes, and we didn't think we'd have any market to sell it as a retail product. Then one of our growing partners and his daughter came up with this simple porridge recipe, which uses the tasty, nutritious semolina from milling in combination with our classic wheat bran. We sell it under the name Farmer's Porridge. It has a bit of a cult following. If you have some, you can use it instead of the farro semolina and wheat bran specified in the recipe.

This is what you want Cream of Wheat to taste like as an adult – creamy and comforting, but with a bit more bite and none of that claggy wallpaper-paste texture. I can barely call this a recipe; it's more of a simple way to start your morning. Use a light touch with the maple syrup and adjust the quantities to suit your palate. Some people find that the farro has enough sweetness on its own and leave it out altogether.

Serves 2

85 g (3 oz/½ cup) farro semolina

1 tablespoon wheat bran

480 ml (16 fl oz/2 cups) water or your choice of milk

1 tablespoon maple syrup

15 g (½ oz/1 tablespoon) almond butter

1 tablespoon golden raisins (sultanas)

heavy (thick/double) cream, to serve

Toast the farro semolina and wheat bran in a saucepan over a low heat for 5 minutes, stirring regularly so it doesn't catch and burn.

Add the water or milk, increase the heat and bring to a boil, stirring constantly, then reduce the heat to low again and simmer for 15 minutes until creamy. Remove from the stove and stir in the maple syrup, almond butter and raisins. Serve warm with a dollop of cream.

Fig & Ricotta Tart

WITH FARRO CRUST

I always dreamed of having my own fig tree. Now I have a fig tree, a lemon tree, two apple trees and an orange tree, and I feel like the richest person in the world. It's a black mission fig and I'm training it to grow against our fence. When they're in season I usually eat the ripe figs straight off the tree, but if any make it into the house I use them in this fancy tart. If you have the same problem of disappearing figs, plums make a great substitute.

Serves 8

12 fresh figs

FARRO CRUST

240 g (8½ oz/1½ cups) Farro Flour

60 g (2 oz/½ cup) powdered (icing) sugar

¼ teaspoon fine sea salt

150 g (5½ oz/10 tablespoons) butter, cut into 1 cm (½ in) cubes

1 egg

RICOTTA FILLING

450 g (1 lb/2 cups) fresh ricotta, well drained

2 eggs

85 g (3 oz/¼ cup) honey

1 vanilla bean, split and seeds scraped, or ½ teaspoon vanilla extract

¼ teaspoon fine sea salt

To make the crust, pulse together the flour, sugar and salt in a food processor. Add the cubes of butter and pulse until crumbly. Add the egg and continue to pulse until the dough starts to clump together. Turn out the dough onto a clean work surface and gently shape into a smooth ball, then wrap it and rest in the fridge for 1 hour (or up to 3 days if you are planning ahead).

Preheat the oven to 190°C (375°F). Butter a 28 cm × 20 cm (11 in × 8 in) rectangular or 23 cm (9 in) round tart pan with a removable base.

Roll out the dough on a well-floured work surface until slightly larger than your prepared pan. Transfer the pastry to the pan and gently press to fit, then trim the edges to neaten. Use a fork to poke a few holes in the crust and bake for 20 minutes.

Meanwhile, to make the filling, mix together all the ingredients in a large bowl until smooth and well combined.

Remove the crust from the oven and pour in the filling. Return the tart to the oven and bake for another 35 minutes, or until the pastry is golden and the ricotta filling is set like a custard.

Allow the tart to cool to room temperature, then gently remove it from the pan, using a knife to loosen the sides where needed. Finely slice the figs and layer them on top, then serve.

Lemon Poppy Seed Shortbread

The farro flour gives this classic Scottish biscuit such a warm and nutty flavor profile – perfect for dunking in a morning cup of coffee. My children love these cookies, so I usually make them with my smallest cookie cutter to keep them kid-sized. Don't be alarmed if this dough is a bit sandy – it's quite normal. And you don't need to be too concerned about overworking the dough either. Keep working it! It'll come together nicely, I promise.

Makes about 24

110 g (4 oz/½ cup) brown sugar

60 g (2 oz/½ cup) powdered (icing) sugar

170 g (6 oz/¾ cup) butter, at room temperature

240 g (8½ oz/1½ cups) Farro Flour

¼ teaspoon fine sea salt

1 tablespoon poppy seeds

grated zest of 1 lemon

Preheat the oven to 150°C (300°F). Line a cookie sheet with parchment (baking) paper or a silicone baking mat.

In the bowl of a stand mixer fitted with the paddle attachment (or food processor), mix together the sugars and butter until combined. Add the flour and salt and pulse or mix into a shaggy dough, then mix in the poppy seeds and lemon zest.

Turn out the dough onto a lightly floured work surface and press into a cohesive ball. Sandwich the dough between two pieces of parchment paper to keep it from sticking, then roll out to a 3 mm (⅛ in) thick disc. Using a 4 cm (1½ in) round cookie cutter (or any shape you like), cut out the cookies and carefully transfer with a spatula to the prepared sheet. Reroll the scraps and cut out a few more to use up all the dough.

Bake for 30 minutes, or until just starting to brown. If you have used a different shape cutter, the baking time might vary so keep an eye on the cookies. Remove and cool completely on a wire rack. Store in an airtight container at room temperature for up to 1 week.

BARLEY

Barley comes in an astonishing array of colors: purple, bronze, black. We've grown all three at the mill in the last ten years, but recently we've settled on the purple barley as a favorite for flavor, novelty, and nutrient density.

Emerging alongside einkorn and farro in the Fertile Crescent, barley has been utilized so much in the making of fodder, food, and drink that it has climbed to fourth place in the ranks of worldwide grain production. Even with such an impressive rise to fame, barley doesn't feature as a star player in the typical American grocery store.

We hoped to highlight the flavor and nutritional value of barley in an easy-to-use product that families could incorporate into their daily rhythms without learning new recipes or baking techniques. When we released our Tibetan Purple Barley Pancake Mix, I thought we'd have a runaway success on our hands. After all, who can resist a food colored purple by nature? Turns out not everyone is keen to start their day with naturally purple pancakes, so we eventually decided to discontinue the product. We only bring it back once a year for the few but fiercely loyal purple food fans. Devoting an entire chapter to this wonderful grain is a kind of personal revenge – my chance to convince anyone and everyone to give this purple barley the attention it deserves.

FLAVOR PROFILE

Purple barley has a cereal taste with tangy citrus undertones.

SUBSTITUTES

If you can't source purple barley, all of the following recipes can be made with other types of barley.

Purple Barley Ginger Cordial

My dad went through a big barley water phase a few years ago. He'd take jugs of his potions to the office for feedback, and unmarked jars of murky liquid would show up in my fridge. He was sure it was the up-and-coming best-selling beverage, the next kombucha or Red Bull, guaranteed to put hair on your chest and cure what ails you. Let's just say this product never made it past R&D.

I was very surprised when I found out later that barley water lemonade is the official drink of Wimbledon – wait, fancy British people drink barley water while watching tennis, like they're in an Oscar Wilde novel? Why didn't anybody tell me? I would have tried much harder to develop a taste for it. It's all in how you sell it, Dad.

To be fair, barley water truly is packed with health benefits and has been used as a medicinal drink in many cultures before it became a posh refreshment. This ginger-honey version is a crowd-pleasing thirst quencher. And I never tire of the disbelief on people's faces when they hear where its bright magenta color comes from.

Makes about 1.4 liters (47 fl oz/6 cups)

200 g (7 oz/1 cup) Tibetan Purple Barley Berries

85 g (3 oz/¼ cup) honey

juice of 2 lemons

5 cm (2 in) piece of ginger, roughly chopped

Rinse the barley, then place in a large saucepan and cover with 2.8 liters (94 fl oz/12 cups) water. Bring to a boil, then reduce the heat and simmer for 50 minutes. Strain and reserve the cooking liquid – it will be a deep purple color. (Save the barley and use it in another dish, such as a barley version of the Harvest Grain Bowl on page 132.)

Return the strained cooking liquid to the pan and add the remaining ingredients. Bring to a boil, then reduce the heat and simmer for 20 minutes, or until the honey has dissolved and the ginger flavor has permeated the liquid.

Remove the pan from the heat and strain out the large pieces of ginger. Pour into clean bottles and chill well before serving over ice. Or pair it with gin for a perfect cocktail. The cordial will keep in the fridge for up to 1 week.

Purple Potato Pierogi

WITH CHIVES

One of my favorite Saturday morning activities is walking with the kids to the Phoenix farmers' market. I load up on veggies and my kids beg for a sourdough pain au chocolat from a local bakery that uses our flour.

We got our start selling our flours at this market, but once local grocery stores started stocking our products we stopped attending the market to focus on our wholesale business. I don't miss the early start on Saturday mornings, but I do miss the camaraderie with customers and fellow stall holders.

In the last few years our local market scene has exploded, and it seems like there's a new vendor to discover every week. I'm so grateful to have a place close by where I can shop for seasonal produce, most of it organically grown, and find surprising fruits and vegetable varietals I never knew existed. There's truly no end to the diversity that nature has to offer. I'm always delighted when I spot new purple potatoes at the market in the spring. With a deep violet flesh and the classic starchy characteristics we expect from potatoes in Eastern European dishes, they add a fun visual twist on the familiar taste we know and love.

Serves 4

60 ml (2 fl oz/4 tablespoons) melted butter

2 tablespoons chopped chives

PIEROGI DOUGH

130 g (4½ oz/1 cup) Tibetan Purple Barley Flour or Bronze Barley Flour

120 g (4½ oz/1 cup) all-purpose (plain) flour

½ teaspoon fine sea salt

1 tablespoon olive oil

POTATO FILLING

455 g (1 lb) purple or yellow potatoes, peeled

75 g (2¾ oz/½ cup) finely chopped sauerkraut

115 g (4 oz/1 cup) farmer's cheese or grated sharp cheddar

To make the dough, mix together the flours and salt in a large bowl. Combine the olive oil and 190 ml (6½ fl oz) warm water in a liquid measuring cup, then pour it into the flour mixture and mix until it comes together to form a ball. Turn out the dough onto a clean work surface and knead for 5 minutes. If the dough is sticking to your work surface, lightly dust the dough with flour and work it in, repeating if it continues to stick. If your dough is too dry and doesn't come together in a cohesive ball, wet your hands and work the moisture into the dough; repeat if the dough continues to crumble. When the dough is smooth and elastic, cover it in airtight wrap and rest at room temperature for 30 minutes.

To prepare the filling, boil the potatoes for about 20 minutes until they are soft and break apart easily with a fork. Drain and mash with a fork (not too finely – you still want a bit of texture), then mix in the sauerkraut and cheese.

Divide the rested dough into four pieces. Work with one piece at a time and keep the rest covered to stop it drying out. On a non-stick pastry mat or lightly floured surface, roll out the dough to a 2 mm (¹/₁₆ in) thickness. Use a 10 cm (4 in) round cookie cutter to cut out rounds and place on a lightly floured tray or board. Cover with a damp tea towel and repeat with the other three pieces of dough, re-rolling the scraps to use up all the dough.

Fill the center of each dough round with a tablespoon of filling and fold the dough over into a semicircle. Seal the edges by pressing them together with a fork. Place the finished pierogi on a piece of parchment (baking) paper or rimmed baking sheet lightly dusted with flour and cover with a tea towel.

Bring a large saucepan of salted water to a boil. Working in two batches so you don't overcrowd the pan, add the pierogi and boil for 2–3 minutes (depending on the thickness of your dough). Remove with a slotted spoon and place on a platter. Toss in the butter and chives and serve warm.

Sprouted Barley Salad

WITH MINT AND BARBERRIES

We are always accidentally sprouting grain at the mill. It's inevitable that wheat spills as we move it about the farm, and little patches of wheat grass emerge from the truck bed or outside the mill's back door. My favorite was the little patch that grew on the farm's forklift, making for a comfy seat cover. Sprouting grains in the kitchen turned out to be just as easy and it unlocks a lovely sweetness. In this salad, the sweetness is balanced out by spicy jalapeños and tangy barberries. I was introduced to barberries by Iranian friends at university. They are like a tiny, more subtle cranberry and I've found that, as with lemon, they can be added to just about everything.

Serves 8 as a side

200 g (7 oz/1 cup) Tibetan Purple Barley Berries (or use black or bronze), sprouted (see page 45 and Tip)

3 tablespoons fresh or dried barberries (see Tip)

½ cup mint leaves, finely chopped

½ cup Italian (flat-leaf) parsley leaves, finely chopped

2 celery stalks, finely chopped

½ jalapeño chili, seeds removed, finely chopped

2 lemon or Persian cucumbers (cukes), roughly chopped

225 g (8 oz) feta, crumbled

60 ml (2 fl oz/¼ cup) olive oil

juice of 1 lemon

1 teaspoon Aleppo pepper

flaky sea salt

Rinse the sprouted barley and place in a large pot with 960 ml (32½ fl oz/4 cups) water. Bring to a boil, then reduce the heat and simmer for 40 minutes, or until the barley is soft and chewy. Drain off the excess water and set aside to cool.

If you have a pressure cooker, you can reduce the cooking time for the sprouted barley. Place the barley and water in the cooker, cover and lock the lid, then set to high pressure for 6 minutes. Manually release the pressure and drain the excess water, then set aside to cool.

Place the cooked barley, barberries, mint, parsley, celery, jalapeño, cucumber and feta in a large bowl. Dress with the olive oil, lemon juice and Aleppo pepper and toss to coat and combine. Sprinkle with flaky salt to taste and serve.

TIPS

As well as bringing out the sweetness of the barley berries, sprouting extracts the nutritional benefits of barley while making it easy on the stomach. Barley is a very high-fiber grain and some people (myself included) find it hard to digest the whole berry. That said, if you don't have time to sprout them, unsprouted berries also work well in this recipe.

Barberries can be found dried or fresh at Middle Eastern markets. If you are using the dried version, plump them up in hot water for 10 minutes first. Cranberries make a good substitute if you can't source barberries.

Breakfast Gua Bao
STEAMED BUNS with SRIRACHA BACON and MICROGREENS

There's a whole world of steamed breads out there – yet another way to transform wheat into something delicious and exploit the magical properties of gluten. These steamed buns were inspired by a customer of the mill whose market stand was built on perfecting these steamed delicacies. I couldn't go to the Saturday farmers' market without feasting on one of their breakfast buns. The recipe requires the dough to rest twice, so allow a good couple of hours for this. There is a bit of technique involved, but the buns are fun to make and will be scooped up at lightning speed by the whole family.

Makes 12

scrambled, fried or poached eggs (however you like them)

½ avocado, finely sliced

handful of microgreens

hot sauce, to serve

GUA BAO

180 ml (6 fl oz/¾ cup) milk, warmed to approximately 45°C (110°F)

1 teaspoon instant dry yeast

240 g (8½ oz/1½ cups) White Sonora Type 00 Flour or all-purpose (plain) flour

65 g (2¼ oz/½ cup) Tibetan Purple Barley Flour or Bronze Barley Flour

1 teaspoon baking powder

1 tablespoon granulated sugar

2 tablespoons olive oil, plus extra for brushing

SRIRACHA BACON

6 slices of bacon, halved crosswise

3 tablespoons maple syrup

1 tablespoon soy sauce

1 tablespoon sriracha/hot sauce

Prepare 12 pieces of parchment (baking) paper, each about 10 cm (4 in) square.

For the gua bao, combine the warm milk and yeast in a small bowl. Place the flours, baking powder and sugar in a large bowl. Pour in the milk mixture, add the olive oil and mix until it comes together in a rough ball. Turn out the dough onto a work surface and knead for about 5 minutes until the texture is smooth and elastic. If the dough is sticking to your work surface, lightly dust it with 1–2 teaspoons extra flour and work it into the dough; repeat if it continues to stick. If your dough is too dry and doesn't form a cohesive ball, wet your hands and work the moisture into the dough. Repeat if the dough continues to crumble. When it is ready, the dough will spring back if you press your finger into it. Place the dough in a large bowl, cover and rest at room temperature for 1½ hours, or until doubled in size.

Punch the dough down to remove large air bubbles, then divide it into 12 even pieces (about 45 g/1½ oz each) and shape them into neat balls. Tuck in the edges so the seam is on the bottom and the top is smooth – this will help the dough roll out more smoothly. Keep the balls of dough covered with a tea towel as you work to prevent them from drying out.

Use a rolling pin or smooth drinking glass to roll the balls into 10 cm × 8 cm (4 in × 3¼ in) ovals. Brush the top lightly with olive oil and fold the dough over into a semi-circle. The oil will stop the two sides of the bun sticking to each other so they open easily for fillings. Place each bun on a prepared piece of parchment paper and place in a two-tier bamboo steamer, six buns per tier. Cover with a tea towel and rest at room temperature for 30 minutes.

Meanwhile, to make the sriracha bacon, preheat the oven to 200°C (400°F) and line a rimmed baking sheet with tinfoil. Place the bacon on the tray in a single layer. In a small bowl, mix together the maple, soy sauce and sriracha and brush over both sides of the bacon. Bake for 30 minutes, or until crispy, flipping the bacon over halfway through.

TIP

If you are making these for brunch and want to prepare them the night before, steam the buns, then allow them to cool completely and store in an airtight container in the fridge. Reheat them in the steamer basket for 5 minutes before serving.

When you are ready to cook the buns, half-fill with water a wide saucepan or wok that will neatly fit your bamboo steamer and bring to a boil. Make sure the water does not touch the bottom of the steamer basket. Reduce to a simmer and steam for 12 minutes. Try to avoid lifting the lid to check on the buns because the condensation will drip down and make them bumpy. Turn off the heat and let the buns rest in the steamer for 5 minutes.

Open the buns and fill with eggs, bacon, avocado and a sprinkling of microgreens. Enjoy them warm.

Purple Barley Scones

WITH PECANS

These scones are quiet and unassuming, but the space created by their simplicity allows the flavor of the purple barley to completely own the spotlight. The taste of barley lingers, and you'll find yourself craving another scone as soon as you've finished your first.

Makes 12

2 eggs

60 ml (2 fl oz/¼ cup) whole (full-cream) milk

60 g (2 oz/¼ cup) heavy (thick/double) cream, plus extra for brushing

325 g (11½ oz/2½ cups) Tibetan Purple Barley Flour or Bronze Barley Flour (though of course the scones won't be purple)

50 g (1¾ oz/¼ cup) granulated sugar

1 teaspoon baking powder

¼ teaspoon fine sea salt

285 g (10 oz/1¼ cups) unsalted butter, diced and chilled

85 g (3 oz/¾ cup) pecans, finely chopped

turbinado or raw sugar, for sprinkling

butter and jam, to serve

Preheat the oven to 175°C (350°F). Line a rimmed baking sheet with parchment (baking) paper.

In a small bowl, whisk together the eggs, milk and cream.

Whisk together the flour, sugar, baking powder and salt in a large bowl. Scatter the butter over the top and rub in with your fingertips to create a coarse crumbly mixture. Don't overmix. It is fine to see bits of butter; you don't want the butter to melt or to be completely incorporated into the dry ingredients.

Add the milk mixture and mix with your hands or a large wooden spoon until just combined. Gently stir in the pecans. Tip onto a floured work surface and lightly knead the dough four times, then gently pat it into a disk about 1 cm (½ in) thick. Using a floured 7.5 cm (3 in) round biscuit cutter, cut out rounds and place on the prepared sheet, leaving a space of about 5 cm (2 in) between each scone. Gently gather the scraps and repeat with the remaining dough.

Lightly brush the top of each scone with extra cream and sprinkle with turbinado or raw sugar. Bake for about 20 minutes, or until golden brown.

Remove from the oven and allow to cool for about 10 minutes before serving. Scones are usually best eaten on the day of baking, but these will keep nicely until the next day if there are any leftovers. Serve with butter and jam.

Chilled Yogurt Barley Soup

WITH HERBS AND CUCUMBER

During my undergrad years, I spent a summer working in Turkey. I loved my time there; so many new experiences, tastes and sounds, and I felt so warmly welcomed by my host family. They shared traditional Turkish foods with me, and I was eager to reciprocate with some of the American dishes I had grown up with. I started with the breakfast diner classic French toast. Unfortunately I mistook their jar of salt for sugar, and it was ... not my finest culinary moment. My sweet little host brother kept insisting it was good and carried on eating, bless his lying heart.

One taste experience that made a lasting impression on me from my time there was a cold cucumber yogurt soup, called cacık. There are many versions of yogurt soup in the Black Sea region, with each culture adapting it slightly to suit their own tastes and traditions. This is my contribution from our region, which I'm hoping brings a little bit of the Sonoran desert to a Turkish classic and a bit of Turkish tradition to the desert.

Serves 6

30 g (1 oz/2 tablespoons) butter

3 small leeks, finely chopped

2 garlic cloves, finely chopped

200 g (7 oz/1 cup) Bronze Barley Berries

960 ml (32½ fl oz/4 cups) chicken stock

2 eggs

1 tablespoon all-purpose (plain) flour

345 g (12 oz/1½ cups) Greek or other plain yogurt

1 tablespoon finely chopped mint

1 tablespoon finely chopped cilantro (coriander)

1 tablespoon chopped chives

2 short or Persian cucumbers (cukes), seeds removed and grated

fine sea salt and freshly ground black pepper

Melt the butter in a medium saucepan over a medium heat and sauté the leek and garlic until softened. Stir in the barley, then cover with the chicken stock. Bring to a boil, then reduce the heat and simmer, covered, for 50 minutes, or until the barley is soft.

Meanwhile, mix together the eggs, flour, yogurt, fresh herbs and cucumber in a bowl.

Take the saucepan off the heat and slowly add the yogurt mixture. Take your time so the warm stock tempers the yogurt and prevents the soup from curdling. Return the pan to a medium heat and warm through, stirring frequently and being careful not to let it boil. As soon as the soup has thickened, take it off the heat. Season to taste with salt and pepper and cool for 15 minutes, then cover and refrigerate. Serve chilled.

Purple Pickled Eggs

When you are draining cooked purple barley, don't throw out the cooking liquid. Its vibrant purple color makes these simple pickled eggs pop.

Makes 6

240 ml (8 fl oz/1 cup) Tibetan Purple Barley Berry cooking liquid

100 g (3½ oz/½ cup) granulated sugar

240 ml (8 fl oz/1 cup) apple-cider vinegar

1 teaspoon fine sea salt

6 hard-boiled eggs, peeled

Combine the barley cooking liquid, sugar, vinegar and salt in a small saucepan over a low heat, bring to a boil and simmer for about 5 minutes until the sugar has dissolved. Remove from the heat and allow to cool for a few minutes.

Place the eggs in a glass jar, then pour in the pickling liquid. Cover and refrigerate for 24 hours before serving. The eggs will keep in the fridge for up to 3 months.

They go well with Farro Furikake (pictured below, recipe on page 92).

Barley Flatbread

WITH NIGELLA AND SESAME SEEDS

Oftentimes, artisanal flour is associated with one particular style of hearth bread – a well-risen, mounded rustic loaf, the Instagram sourdough shot, something straight out of a French boulangerie. While I love my classic European loaves, we can't neglect the wonderful world of flatbreads. This version draws on flavors and traditions from Persia, India and Tibet. The barley flour makes these flavorful enough to be eaten on their own, but my favorite pairing is with scrambled eggs for brunch.

Makes 4 large flatbreads

2 teaspoons instant dry yeast

1 tablespoon vegetable oil

1 teaspoon fine sea salt

1½ tablespoons granulated sugar

120 ml (4 fl oz/½ cup) whole (full-cream) milk

130 g (4½ oz/1 cup) Bronze Barley Flour

120 g (4½ oz/1 cup) all-purpose (plain) flour

melted butter or olive oil, for brushing

½ tablespoon nigella seeds

½ tablespoon sesame seeds

Lightly oil a large mixing bowl and set aside.

In the bowl of a stand mixer fitted with the dough hook, combine the yeast, vegetable oil, salt, sugar, milk and 120 ml (4 fl oz/½ cup) water and mix on low speed. Add the flours and mix on medium speed until it forms a shaggy ball. Switch the mixer off and allow the dough to rest for 20–30 minutes.

Turn out the dough onto a lightly floured work surface and knead for 4–6 minutes until smooth and elastic. Place the dough in the oiled bowl, cover and allow to proof for 1 hour, or until it has doubled in size.

Divide the dough into four even pieces and roll each one into a long oval. Place on a baking sheet lined with parchment (baking) paper, cover loosely and rest at room temperature for 45 minutes.

Preheat the oven to 260°C (500°F).

Bake the breads for 2–3 minutes, then flip them over and bake for another 2–3 minutes until they are golden and slightly puffed. Remove from the oven, brush the tops with butter or olive oil and sprinkle with the nigella and sesame seeds. Enjoy warm.

Creamy Barley Salmon Salad

WITH ASPARAGUS AND FENNEL

Because barley is the first crop to ripen in the spring it has become a symbol of new life and hope, making it the perfect grain for this vibrant springtime salad.

Serves 6

200 g (7 oz/1 cup) Tibetan Purple or Bronze Barley Berries

2 × 115 g (4 oz) salmon fillets, skin removed and pin-boned

1 bunch asparagus, ends trimmed, chopped into large pieces

1 fennel bulb, finely sliced

2 tablespoons olive oil

4 radishes, finely sliced

fennel fronds, to garnish (optional)

CREAMY DILL DRESSING

115 g (4 oz/½ cup) sour cream

115 g (4 oz/½ cup) mayonnaise

1 shallot, finely chopped

juice of 1 lemon

3 tablespoons chopped dill

3 tablespoons Dijon mustard

fine sea salt and freshly ground black pepper

Rinse the barley, then place in a medium saucepan and cover with 715 ml (24 fl oz/3 cups) water. Bring to a boil, then reduce the heat and simmer for 45 minutes until the barley is soft and chewy. Drain.

Preheat the oven to 220°C (425°F).

Place the salmon, asparagus and fennel on a sheet pan (baking sheet) and drizzle with the olive oil. Roast for 12 minutes, or until the salmon is cooked and the asparagus and fennel are tender. The time will vary slightly depending on the thickness of your salmon fillets – use a knife to check for opaque pinkness. Remove and set aside to cool, then flake the salmon into bite-sized pieces.

To make the dressing, combine all the ingredients in a small bowl.

Toss together the cooked barley, flaked salmon, asparagus, fennel, radish and dressing in a large bowl. Place in the fridge and serve chilled, garnished with fennel fronds, if desired.

EINKORN

If modern flour is like streaming music from a Bluetooth speaker, then ancient grains are like pumping out the classics on a turntable. Inconvenient and antiquated, yet I just can't seem to let this clunky piece of technology go. Just like I'm convinced ancient grains taste better, I'm convinced 'Space Oddity' sounds better on my record player, with all its crackles and pops. Or maybe it's just that I've taken the time to sit down and really listen, fully engaged in the process of setting the needle and flipping the record over. An intentional moment requiring my full attention rather than background noise, algorithmically shuffled to fill the empty space.

Einkorn is the food of our ancestors. It is a slender, petite grain, far less genetically complex than bread wheat, that still bears a close resemblance to the wild grasses it evolved from. If you look closely at the individual einkorn berries, you will notice they are missing the medial crevice that most wheat berries have. An uncooked einkorn berry is soft enough to pop straight into your mouth, like a sunflower seed. It fell out of favor because, just as with farro, it has an extra casing around its seeds called a hull, which requires a special processing step to remove. Humans spent hundreds of years cultivating wheat that did not have this hull, making it easier to both grow and mill. And yet here we are, reviving this ancient wheat, seeking out equipment that is no longer even made in the United States to remove the hull, all for a small taste of its anachronistic goodness.

Einkorn is so high maintenance that we always mill it as whole wheat, so no part of the grain is lost. It's one of our most expensive flours. And yet, for all its fussiness, if I had to pick one flour to nourish me while I was stuck on a desert island, it would be einkorn flour. It has the comforting taste of wisdom – a grain that has seen it all and has been feeding humans for more than 10,000 years. With its rounded, utterly complete flavor, I like to think of it as the sum of all the other grains that came after it.

FLAVOR PROFILE

Einkorn is full-bodied with a gentle herbiness and undertones of vanilla.

Sprouted Einkorn Parfait

WITH WHIPPED VANILLA YOGURT

Sprouting is a way to unlock the sugars and proteins in grains and make them more digestible. The process can take a couple of days, so this recipe requires a little planning ahead. These parfaits can be prepared the night before and pulled out of the fridge the next morning for a quick and nourishing start to your day. If pears are not in season, blueberries make a great substitute.

Serves 4

100 g (3½ oz/½ cup) Einkorn Berries, sprouted (see page 45)

2 tablespoons honey

½ teaspoon ground cinnamon, plus extra to garnish

2 pears, halved, cored and cut into small pieces

2 tablespoons toasted pepitas (pumpkin seeds)

WHIPPED VANILLA YOGURT

115 g (4 oz/½ cup) Greek yogurt

115 g (4 oz/½ cup) heavy (thick/double) cream

1 tablespoon granulated sugar

½ teaspoon vanilla extract

pinch of fine sea salt

Place the sprouted einkorn berries and 240 ml (8 fl oz/1 cup) water in a small saucepan. Bring to a boil, then reduce the heat and simmer for 35 minutes, or until the water has been absorbed and the berries are soft and chewy. If the berries are not soft enough or the water cooks off too quickly, add another 60 ml (2 fl oz/¼ cup) water and cook for a bit longer. Set aside to cool.

If you have a pressure cooker, you can reduce the cooking time. Place the sprouted einkorn and 960 ml (32½ fl oz/4 cups) water in the cooker, cover and lock the lid, then set to high pressure for 6 minutes. Manually release the pressure and drain the excess water, then set aside to cool.

Meanwhile, to make the whipped yogurt, use a handheld electric beater or stand mixer fitted with the whisk attachment to whip together all the ingredients until stiff peaks form.

Mix together the cooled einkorn, honey and cinnamon.

You can assemble the parfaits in individual glasses or one large bowl. All you need to do is layer the einkorn mixture, pear and whipped yogurt. Finish with a final dollop of whipped yogurt and garnish with the pepitas and a sprinkle of cinnamon.

Chill in the fridge for at least 20 minutes before serving.

Einkorn Blondies

WITH WHITE CHOCOLATE AND RASPBERRIES

To combat any notions of heritage grains being overly austere or boring,
I wanted to include a truly decadent recipe in this book: a perfect rich and
chewy blondie, topped with white chocolate and raspberries to push it
right over the edge.

Makes 16

280 g (10 oz/2 cups) Einkorn Flour

1½ teaspoons baking powder

¼ teaspoon fine sea salt

160 g (5½ oz/11 tablespoons) unsalted butter, at room temperature

300 g (10½ oz/1⅓ cup) brown sugar

2 eggs

1 teaspoon vanilla extract

85 g (3 oz/½ cup) white chocolate chips

125 g (4½ oz/1 cup) raspberries

Preheat the oven to 175°C (350°F). Grease a 20 cm (8 in) square baking pan and line the base with parchment (baking) paper, leaving an overhang on two sides to help lift out the brownie later.

In a large bowl, whisk together the flour, baking powder and salt. Set aside.

In the bowl of a stand mixer fitted with the paddle attachment, cream the butter and brown sugar until pale and fluffy. Add the eggs one at a time and mix until thoroughly incorporated. Mix in the vanilla.

Scrape down the side of the bowl with a spatula, then gradually add the flour mixture. Mix on the lowest speed until the flour is just incorporated. Be careful not to overmix the batter as this will incorporate too much air and cause the middle to sink during baking. Scrape the base of the bowl to ensure there are no lumps of dry ingredients remaining.

Scoop the batter into the prepared pan and smooth the surface. Arrange the chocolate chips and raspberries evenly over the top and gently press into the batter. Place the pan on the middle rack of the oven and bake for 50–55 minutes until the edges are brown and the middle is set but still slightly molten. Remove from the oven and cool in the pan for 20 minutes, then use the overhanging parchment paper to carefully lift out the blondie.

Cut into squares and serve. Store leftover blondies in an airtight container at room temperature for 2–3 days, or wrap them individually and freeze for up to 3 months.

Einkorn Waffles

During the long sleepless nights of newborn haze and breastfeeding-induced hunger, I made a terrible (and expensive) discovery: I could use my phone to order breakfast and have it delivered to my doorstep at first light. The thought of a syrup-soaked waffle (even if it was cold by the time it arrived) helped me make it through another night without sleep. Eventually, nights and days righted themselves and I was able to put my phone down and make the waffles myself. Before long, my little sleep-stealer was enjoying them too.

There are endless clever variations on waffles, but for me, a plain Belgian-style waffle with butter and warm maple syrup will always win the day. The only enhancement in this recipe is the flavor of the einkorn, which really holds its own. Give it a try, and watch einkorn waffles become a new weekend tradition.

Makes 8

245 g (8½ oz/1¾ cups) Einkorn Flour

½ teaspoon fine sea salt

2 tablespoons granulated sugar

2 teaspoons baking soda (bicarbonate of soda)

1 teaspoon ground cinnamon

½ teaspoon freshly grated nutmeg

345 g (12 oz/1½ cups) Greek yogurt

120 ml (4 fl oz/½ cup) whole (full-cream) milk or almond milk

2 eggs, separated

60 ml (2 fl oz/4 tablespoons) melted butter, plus extra butter to serve

½ teaspoon vanilla extract

neutral oil, for brushing

maple syrup, to serve

In a large bowl, combine the flour, salt, sugar, baking soda, cinnamon and nutmeg.

In a separate bowl, mix together the yogurt, milk, egg yolks, melted butter and vanilla. Add to the dry ingredients and mix well.

Using a stand mixer fitted with the whisk attachment or a handheld electric beater, beat the egg whites until stiff peaks form, then gently fold them into the batter. The batter will be thick and streaked with the egg white.

Lightly brush the waffle iron with oil. Scoop enough batter onto the iron to just cover it and cook according to the manufacturer's instructions until crisp and golden, about 5 minutes. Repeat with the remaining batter. Serve warm with butter and maple syrup.

Aunt Sadie's Einkorn Tabbouleh

Growing up, we were lucky to have access to a huge variety of foods, courtesy of our Japanese neighbor, international exchange homestay students, nutritionist mother and Armenian adopted godmother, Aunt Sadie. This is an einkorn berry update of Aunt Sadie's tabbouleh recipe, for which she generously gave me her blessing. However, she will not be pleased about my lack of attention to the parsley. When I was a child, my one solemn kitchen task was to pick each individual leaf off the stalk, ensuring the finished salad wasn't sullied by pesky stems. But these days, seriously who has the time? Unless you have willing child labor at the ready, I suggest giving your bunch of parsley a quick haircut, then chopping the leaves and stems as finely as you can. No need to tell Aunt Sadie.

Serves 6 as a side

100 g (3½ oz/½ cup) Einkorn Berries (see Tip)

1 bunch curly parsley, stems removed

60 ml (2 fl oz/¼ cup) olive oil

2 tablespoons lemon juice

2 scallions (spring onions), finely sliced

1 tablespoon Aleppo pepper

½ teaspoon finely chopped mint

½ teaspoon fine sea salt

1 large tomato, diced

Place the einkorn berries and 240 ml (8 fl oz/1 cup) water in a small saucepan. Bring to a boil, then reduce the heat and simmer for 35 minutes, or until the water has been absorbed and the berries are soft and chewy. If the berries are not soft enough or the water cooks off too quickly, add another 60 ml (2 fl oz/¼ cup) water and cook for a bit longer. Set aside to cool.

If you have a pressure cooker, you can reduce the cooking time for this recipe. Place the einkorn berries and 480 ml (16 fl oz/ 2 cups) water in the cooker, cover and lock the lid, then set to high pressure for 15 minutes. Manually release the pressure and drain the excess water, then set aside to cool.

Process the parsley in a food processor until it is very finely chopped, but not a paste (or you can do this with a knife).

Transfer the parsley to a medium serving bowl, add the olive oil, lemon juice and scallion and whisk to combine. Add the einkorn berries, Aleppo pepper, mint and salt and toss well, then place in the fridge to chill. Add the tomato right before serving.

TIP

This salad would taste really good with sprouted einkorn as well. See page 45 for sprouting instructions.

Rainbow Einkorn Berry Slaw

WITH MINT AND APPLES

Colorful and balanced with bright flavors, this recipe makes enough to invite your neighbors for a summer backyard cookout.

Serves 8

100 g (3½ oz/½ cup) Einkorn Berries

2 small beets (preferably red and orange), peeled and cut into thin matchsticks

1 green apple, cored and cut into thin matchsticks

½ small red cabbage, shredded

CREAMY LEMON DRESSING

115 g (4 oz/½ cup) Greek yogurt

115 g (4 oz/½ cup) mayonnaise

juice of ½ lemon, or to taste

1 tablespoon finely chopped mint

½ teaspoon fine sea salt

Place the einkorn berries and 240 ml (8 fl oz/1 cup) water in a small saucepan. Bring to a boil, then reduce the heat and simmer for 35 minutes, or until the water has been absorbed and the berries are soft and chewy. If the berries are not soft enough or the water cooks off too quickly, add another 60 ml (2 fl oz/¼ cup) water and cook for a bit longer. Set aside to cool.

If you have a pressure cooker, you can reduce the cooking time for this recipe. Place the einkorn berries and 960 ml (32½ fl oz/4 cups) water in the cooker, cover and lock the lid, then set to high pressure for 15 minutes. Manually release the pressure and drain the excess water, then set aside to cool.

To make the dressing, combine all the ingredients in a large bowl.

Add the einkorn berries, beet, apple and cabbage to the bowl and toss to coat well with the dressing. Place in the fridge to chill before serving.

Einkorn Beet Ravioli

WITH TOASTED POPPY SEED BUTTER SAUCE

When I first thought about writing a book about grains, I was determined
not to let it become a study in browns – boring and beige. While we take
our grains pretty seriously around the mill, I've always cooked at home
with the belief that food can be fun. I love bright colors; red shoes,
red lipstick and eating a rainbow of food makes me happy, and I enjoy
finding playful ways to make it pretty as well as delicious.

Which neatly brings us to these ravioli, which are downright gorgeous.
Called Casunziei all'Ampezzana in their native Northern Italy,
these translucent parcels of pink beets are sprinkled with blue poppy
seeds. Here, the toasted poppy seeds and einkorn play on the same sweet,
earthy notes, and the beetroot fits right in. This is a beautiful dish to
share at a dinner party.

Serves 6

115 g (4 oz/½ cup) butter

2 tablespoons poppy seeds

grated zest of 1 lemon

PASTA DOUGH

245 g (8½ oz/1¾ cups) Einkorn
Flour

3 eggs

BEET FILLING

2 large red beets, peeled and cut
into 2.5 cm (1 in) cubes

115 g (4 oz/½ cup) fresh ricotta,
well drained

2 egg yolks

2 garlic cloves, finely chopped

¼ teaspoon fine sea salt

To make the pasta dough, tip the flour into a large bowl and
make a small well in the center. Add the eggs to the well and
whisk with a fork, gradually incorporating more flour. Continue to
mix until the flour is hydrated and the dough comes together into
a ball. Turn out the dough onto a lightly floured work surface and
knead for 5 minutes, or until the dough is smooth and elastic.

If the dough is sticking to your work surface, lightly dust it with
1–2 teaspoons extra flour and work it into the dough; repeat if
it continues to stick. If your dough is too dry and doesn't form
a cohesive ball, wet your hands and work the moisture into
the dough. Repeat if the dough continues to crumble. Wrap the
dough in airtight wrap and let it rest at room temperature for
30 minutes or in the fridge for no more than 24 hours.

To make the beet filling, place the beet cubes in a small
saucepan of water and bring to a boil, then reduce the heat
and simmer for about 25 minutes until they are soft and can
be easily pierced with a fork. Drain.

Use a stick blender or food processor to combine the beet,
ricotta, egg yolks, garlic and salt to form a smooth puree. For
best results, the filling should be as dry as possible. To remove
any excess liquid, scoop the filling into a fine mesh sieve or piece
of cheesecloth or muslin and drain over a bowl for 10 minutes.

When you are ready to assemble the ravioli, get out your pasta
machine and divide the pasta dough into four pieces. Work with
one piece at a time and keep the remaining dough covered so it
doesn't dry out. Set your pasta roller to the largest setting and
feed the dough through. Fold the sheet like an envelope and
feed it through the roller several more times. Reduce the setting
size and feed the dough through once, dusting with extra flour
as you go to keep it from sticking. Continue rolling, reducing

the setting size each time, until the dough is so thin it's see-through; usually the second last setting of the pasta machine. To check, hold up the sheet of dough and place your hand behind it; if you can see your hand, it's ready.

Using a 10 cm (4 in) round cookie cutter, cut out as many circles as you can from the sheet of pasta dough. Fill each circle with a scant tablespoon of the beet filling. Fold the dough over the filling to form a semi-circle and seal the edges with a fork. Place the finished ravioli on a lightly floured baking sheet. Repeat with the remaining pieces of dough and filling.

When they are all assembled, bring a large saucepan of salted water to the boil and cook the ravioli for 3–5 minutes until al dente. Drain.

Meanwhile, melt the butter in a small saucepan over a low heat, add the poppy seeds and cook for 2 minutes, or until the butter starts to brown and the poppy seeds are lightly toasted.

Pour the butter poppy sauce over the ravioli and gently toss to coat. Sprinkle with the grated lemon zest and serve warm.

Saffron Chicken Tagine

WITH EINKORN AND FRENCH LENTILS

This cozy one-pot meal is inspired by a traditional Moroccan tagine, although here we have replaced the usual couscous with einkorn berries and lentils. It's the perfect dinner for a chilly autumn evening, and I hope it's a recipe you will come back to again and again.

Serves 6

60 ml (2 fl oz/¼ cup) olive oil

900 g (2 lb) boneless chicken thighs, skin on

1 onion, finely sliced

pinch of saffron threads

½ teaspoon ground ginger

½ teaspoon garlic powder

1 teaspoon sweet paprika

1 cinnamon stick

100 g (3½ oz/½ cup) Einkorn Berries

100 g (3½ oz/½ cup) French (puy) lentils

480 ml (16 fl oz/2 cups) chicken stock

180 g (6½ oz/1 cup) pitted green olives, halved

100 g (3½ oz/½ cup) quartered dried apricots (unsulphured)

1 tablespoon preserved lemon paste or 1 preserved lemon, rind only, chopped

Italian (flat-leaf) parsley, to garnish (optional)

Preheat the oven to 190°C (375°F).

Heat the olive oil in a Dutch oven over a medium heat. Brown the chicken thighs on both sides, then remove the chicken and set aside on a plate. Add the onion and spices and sauté for 5 minutes until fragrant and the onion is translucent. Stir in the einkorn berries, lentils and stock. Cover and place in the oven for 25 minutes.

Remove the Dutch oven from the oven and stir in the olives, apricots and preserved lemon. Nestle the chicken thighs into the lentils and einkorn mixture.

Increase the temperature to 220°C (425°F), then return the tagine to the oven and bake uncovered for another 30 minutes, or until the chicken is cooked through and the tops are browned and crispy. Serve garnished with parsley, if desired.

Dolmas Pie

WITH LAMB, MINT AND EINKORN

This dish is a less labor-intensive take on individual stuffed grape leaves: a fragrant lamb and feta pie, encased in grape leaves and filo pastry. The einkorn takes the place of the traditional rice element for a nice textural update. The method of using a Bundt pan is definitely unconventional and when the final pie is sliced up, it loosely resembles a beef wellington with the meat filling encased in pastry. Labneh, a tangy strained yogurt, is a wonderful foil for the richness of the lamb, but you could simply use Greek yogurt in its place.

Serves 8

200 g (7 oz/1 cup) Einkorn Berries

1 × 400 g (14 oz) jar grape leaves (you will need 30–35 leaves)

2 tablespoons olive oil

1 onion, diced

450 g (1 lb) ground (minced) lamb

1 × 400 g (14 oz) can diced tomatoes, including the liquid

225 g (8 oz) feta, crumbled

35 g (1¼ oz/¼ cup) currants

1 tablespoon dried mint

1 tablespoon Aleppo pepper

1½ teaspoons sumac

360 g (12½ oz) filo pastry, thawed

60 ml (2 fl oz/4 tablespoons) melted butter, plus extra, for greasing

labneh, to serve

Place the einkorn berries and 480 ml (16 fl oz/2 cups) water in a small saucepan. Bring to a boil, then reduce the heat and simmer for 35 minutes, or until the water has been absorbed and the berries are soft and chewy. If the berries are not soft enough or the water cooks off too quickly, add another 60 ml (2 fl oz/¼ cup) water and cook for a bit longer. Set aside to cool.

Preheat the oven to 175°C (350°F).

Rinse the grape leaves and gently separate them, then lay them on a clean tea towel to dry.

Heat the olive oil in a skillet or frying pan over a medium heat, add the onion and sauté until translucent. Add the lamb and cook until browned all over, breaking up any clumps with the back of your wooden spoon. Stir in the tomatoes, feta, currants, dried mint, Aleppo pepper and sumac. Reduce the heat to low and simmer for 20 minutes, or until thickened and most of the liquid has evaporated. Remove the pan from the heat and stir in the cooked einkorn.

Grease the inside of a 25 cm (10 in) Bundt pan. Line with a sheet of filo pastry so that it follows the shape of the pan, including the middle chimney. Brush the pastry with melted butter, then carry on lining the pan with another three sheets of pastry, brushing each one with butter as you go. This is a very forgiving process, so don't worry if the dough cracks. Now line the pastry with a layer of grape leaves, leaving about one-third of the leaves for the top.

Carefully spoon the lamb and einkorn filling into the prepared pan and smooth the surface. Cover with an even layer of the remaining grape leaves, followed by four sheets of filo, brushing each one with butter as before and tucking it in to fit if needed.

Bake for 45 minutes. Place a large serving plate face down on the Bundt pan and carefully invert the pie onto the plate. Let it rest for 15 minutes, then cut into it with a serrated knife and serve with dollops of labneh.

Einkorn Fig Crispbread

I love these nourishing Norwegian crackers. Jammed with seeds, with a heavy emphasis on sesame, they are beautifully bound together with einkorn flour. Serve with a range of cheeses and your favorite mustard.

Makes about 24

70 g (2½ oz/½ cup) Einkorn Flour

40 g (1½ oz/¼ cup) sesame seeds

30 g (1 oz/¼ cup) sunflower seeds

30 g (1 oz/¼ cup) pepitas (pumpkin seeds)

100 g (3½ oz/½ cup) roughly chopped dried figs (about 6–7)

2 tablespoons flax seeds (linseeds)

1 tablespoon honey

¼ teaspoon fine sea salt

Preheat the oven to 150°C (300°F).

In a large bowl, mix together all the ingredients and 60 ml (2 fl oz/¼ cup) water to form a rough, sticky dough. Turn out the dough onto a piece of parchment (baking) paper and place another piece on top, then roll it out to a 6 mm (¼ in) thickness. Rolling the dough between two pieces of paper will keep it from sticking to the rolling pin.

Still on the paper, transfer the dough to a large baking sheet. Lift off the top piece of paper and bake for 10 minutes. Remove from the oven and use a sharp knife to score into 7.5 cm (3 in) square crackers. Bake for another 40 minutes until the crackers are crisp and golden.

Allow to cool completely – they will crisp up even more as they cool. Using the score lines as a guide, break the crispbread into crackers and serve. Leftovers will keep in an airtight container for up to 1 week.

Harvest Grain Bowls

This recipe is inspired by my little brother. Sam is ten years younger than me. He's a good kid and helps with the harvest every summer (mainly to work on his tan, he says). In his days as a frugal college student, he always gathered up the spilled grains from the grain truck and took them home with him for an abundance of free meals. Just to be clear, we do pay him for his seasonal help, but I suppose you could call this a 'perk' of any sort of farm work.

I admire his modern-day gleaning, especially in this age of food excess and waste. One way to enter into this sustainable spirit at home is to pull out all your half-empty jars, boxes and bags of grains – you know, the quarter cup of farro that won't do for a full serving and that mystery jar of odds and ends right up the back – then throw them all in a bowl and make this recipe.

Serves 6

200 g (7 oz/1 cup) Einkorn Berries (or other mixed wheat berries)

60 ml (2 fl oz/¼ cup) soy sauce

1 tablespoon sriracha

1 × 400 g (14 oz) packet firm tofu, pressed and drained

1 head cauliflower, cut into bite-sized florets

1 × 400 g (14 oz) can chickpeas, drained and rinsed

2 tablespoons olive oil

1 avocado, finely sliced

50 g (1¾ oz) microgreens or sprouts

30 g (1 oz/¼ cup) pepitas (pumpkin seeds)

DRESSING

240 ml (8 fl oz/1 cup) coconut milk

115 g (4 oz/1 cup) raw cashews

½ jalapeño chili, seeds removed

juice of 1 lemon

½ cup packed cilantro (coriander) leaves

½ teaspoon fine sea salt

Place the einkorn berries and 480 ml (16 fl oz/2 cups) water in a small saucepan. Bring to a boil, then reduce the heat and simmer for 35 minutes, or until the water has been absorbed and the berries are soft and chewy. If the berries are not soft enough or the water cooks off too quickly, add another 60 ml (2 fl oz/¼ cup) water and cook for a bit longer. Set aside to cool.

If you have a pressure cooker, you can reduce the cooking time for this recipe. Place the einkorn berries and 960 ml (32½ fl oz/ 4 cups) water in the cooker, cover and lock the lid, then set to high pressure for 15 minutes. Manually release the pressure and drain the excess water, then set aside to cool.

Meanwhile, combine the soy sauce and sriracha in a small bowl. Cut the tofu into 1.5 cm (½ in) thick triangles and toss with the soy and sriracha sauce, then leave to marinate at room temperature for 30 minutes.

Preheat the oven to 200°C (400°F).

Toss the cauliflower and chickpeas in the olive oil. Spread out in a roasting pan, along with the drained tofu, and roast for 40 minutes, or until the cauliflower is soft and lightly charred, the chickpeas are crispy, and the tofu is dark and firm.

To make the dressing, blend all the ingredients in a food processor until smooth and creamy.

To assemble the grain bowl, start with a layer of cooked einkorn berries, followed by the tofu, roasted cauliflower and chickpeas, avocado slices, microgreens or sprouts and pepitas. Pour over the dressing and serve.

CORN

A monsoon was imminent, and the corn had to be harvested. If it got wet, there was a high chance it would mold. We furiously picked heads of corn, filling the back of the truck, racing against the black clouds, until my brother backed the Silverado into an irrigation ditch. My sister and I kept moving down rows of corn that were heads taller than us, plucking ears of corn, while my dad and brother tried to unstick the truck.

In 2013, an urban farmer had lent us 5 acres of land and we grew a type of heritage dent corn called Floriani Red. The seed cost a small fortune, and as we husked each ear of corn, we discovered that they had already been eaten through by worms. To add insult to injury, the small amount of the crop that the worms had left for us was covered in a mold that made it inedible. Later that day, our neighbor from Mexico pointed out that we had done everything wrong according to traditional knowledge of corn farming. We were appropriately humbled by the whole experience. Being slow to learn our lesson, we attempted a few more seasons of growing heritage corns with farmers in Arizona and Mexico, all failed crops.

The corn is a funny story of our stubbornness and naiveté, but also a reminder that it's not just the seeds for these heritage varieties that are being lost, but the knowledge surrounding how to grow them. As GMO corn has replaced traditional corn in Mexico, the intricate knowledge of how to tend these seeds is at risk of disappearing within a generation.

Genetic modification is not yet a major concern for wheat, but 92 percent of all corn planted in the US is now genetically modified. One of the few remaining sources of non-GMO corn in the US is grown by the Ute Nation, where we now source our yellow corn.

I wish I could say we grew a whole rainbow of heritage corn varieties – luckily there are other millers devoted to just this cause. If you get hooked on the taste of freshly stone-milled polenta, seek out these rarer varieties with names like Bloody Butcher, Oaxacan Green or Jimmy Red, to name a few.

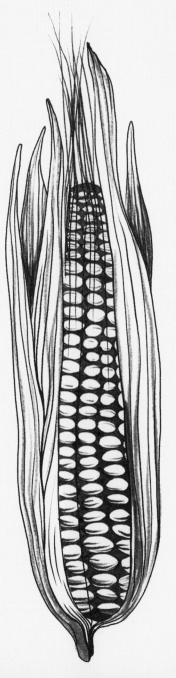

FLAVOR PROFILE

Freshly milled corn tastes bright and sweet and has a milky, starchy texture.

Chocolate Polenta Pudding Cake

The first cookbook I ever owned was *Roald Dahl's Revolting Recipes*. My siblings and I cooked every recipe in that book, each more brilliant and imaginative than the last, but the one we made over and over again was Bruce Bogtrotter's Chocolate Cake from the pages of *Matilda*. A nearly flourless cake with egg whites, it was most definitely a technical challenge, and my siblings and I destroyed the kitchen in the process, using every available bowl and utensil. In spite of the chaos, we were learning the basics of baking: separating eggs, whipping the whites into a flurry and gently folding them into a batter. It also planted the seeds of learning how to be a good host, the glittering feeling it gave us to delight our birthday party guests with a decadent cake. Just as importantly, if less glitteringly, we also learned how to clean up afterwards. This cake would be sure to tempt Bruce Bogtrotter. It's somehow airy and light and rich and pudding-like all at once, with a little extra texture courtesy of the softened polenta.

Serves 8

1 teaspoon fine sea salt

75 g (2¾ oz/½ cup) polenta

225 g (8 oz/1 cup) unsalted butter

225 g (8 oz) dark chocolate, roughly chopped

20 g (¾ oz/¼ cup) cocoa powder

6 eggs

250 g (9 oz/1¼ cups) granulated sugar

1 teaspoon vanilla extract

powdered (icing) sugar, for dusting

Preheat the oven to 175°C (350°F). Lightly oil and line the base of a 23 cm (9 in) springform cake pan. Set aside.

Pour 480 ml (16 fl oz/2 cups) water into a medium saucepan, add the salt and bring to a boil over a medium–high heat. Add the polenta and cook, stirring frequently to prevent it from sticking to the base of the pan. Continue cooking for about 20 minutes until most of the water has been absorbed.

Remove from the heat and add the butter and chocolate. Allow to sit for about 5 minutes, then stir until melted and well combined. Mix in the cocoa powder and set aside.

In the bowl of a stand mixer fitted with the whisk attachment, whip the eggs and sugar until tripled in volume. Gently fold half the mixture into the chocolate polenta, then fold in the rest until no traces of egg are visible, taking care not to overmix. Add the vanilla and give the mixture a quick stir to incorporate.

Transfer the batter to the prepared pan and smooth the surface. Bake for 30–40 minutes, or until the top is dry and somewhat souffléd, with a bit of a jiggle in the center. Remove from the oven and run a thin paring knife around the inside of the pan, then allow to cool completely at room temperature. The cake will sink slightly in the center as it cools. Place the cake in the fridge overnight before releasing the side and removing it from the pan.

Use a sharp thin-bladed knife to cut the cake into slices, wiping the blade between cuts for a clean finish. Finish with a light dusting of powdered sugar and serve. The cake will keep in an airtight container in the fridge for up to 3 days.

Almond Cornmeal Cake

This was one of the first recipes I made with our own product. When I tasted it, I was instantly convinced that the work we were doing was indeed worthwhile. The flavor was an eye opener – bright and summery, with none of the rancid, bitter taste that I had always disliked in cornbread. And now that I understand the production process, I can see why.

If you pay attention to the cornmeal you purchase from the store, you'll notice the word 'degerminated' on most commercial products. It's often stated positively, as though marketing an added asset, when in fact this term just means the most flavorful part of the corn has been removed to extend the shelf life. We leave the germ in the corn, preserving the full flavor and nutrition of the grain, and this is what gives this cake its sweet, buttery taste. And forget the shelf life; the best place to store our cornmeal and polenta is in the freezer.

The ground almonds give this cake just the right amount of crunch. You are allowed to eat it for breakfast, enjoy it with an afternoon cup of coffee, or call it cornbread and serve it warm with a really spicy chili, letting the sweetness of the corn balance out the heat.

Makes 1 loaf

105 g (3½ oz/¾ cup) yellow cornmeal

30 g (1 oz/¼ cup) all-purpose (plain) flour

1 teaspoon baking powder

½ teaspoon fine sea salt

95 g (3¼ oz/¾ cup) raw almonds

150 g (5½ oz/¾ cup) granulated sugar

60 g (2 oz/4 tablespoons) unsalted butter, at room temperature

115 g (4 oz/½ cup) Greek yogurt

3 eggs

½ teaspoon almond extract

Preheat the oven to 165°C (325°F). Butter a loaf (bar) pan or line the base with parchment (baking) paper, leaving an overhang on the two long sides to help lift the cake out easily.

In a large bowl, whisk together the cornmeal, flour, baking powder and salt.

Finely grind the almonds and 100 g (3½ oz/½ cup) of the sugar in a food processor, then stir into the cornmeal mixture.

In the bowl of a stand mixer fitted with the paddle attachment, beat the butter, yogurt and remaining sugar on medium speed until well combined. Beat in the eggs, one at a time, until just incorporated, then beat in the almond extract (the mixture will look curdled, but don't worry). Fold in the cornmeal mixture until just combined.

Pour the batter into the prepared pan and smooth the surface. Bake on the middle rack of the oven for 1 hour, or until a skewer inserted in the center comes out clean. Cool in the pan for 5 minutes, then loosen the edges with a knife and carefully lift the cake onto a wire rack to cool completely. Any leftover cake will keep in an airtight container at room temperature for up to 2 days.

The Miller's Shrimp & Grits

Diego is our current head miller and we hope he will be for many years to come. He's a treasure to work with, and his contribution to our milling operation has been indispensable. On top of that, he's a very talented chef and eventually plans to open his own restaurant, so I know we'll have to let him go some day.

At a recent miller's lunch (our version of a staff lunch where my dad and I cook for everyone) we asked everyone to nominate their favorite comfort food. Most people opted for the usual suspects, like lasagna and warm cheesy dishes, but Diego surprised us all by saying *shrimp*! He grew up by the sea in Mexico and, to him, that's the food of home. I loved his answer so much that I asked if he'd share his comforting shrimp dish in this book. Having tried it, I think it could easily become everyone's new go-to.

Serves 4

960 ml (32½ fl oz/4 cups) chicken stock

fine sea salt or flakes

150 g (5½ oz/1 cup) polenta

45 g (1½ oz/3 tablespoons) butter

good splash of olive oil

½ red onion, finely diced

1 poblano chili pepper, seeds and veins removed, finely chopped (see Tip)

3 garlic cloves, finely chopped

3 roma (plum) tomatoes, finely diced

450 g (1 lb) raw shrimp (prawns), peeled and deveined

freshly ground black pepper

1 bunch cilantro (coriander), leaves picked and chopped

Place the chicken stock and a pinch of salt in a large saucepan over a medium heat. Cover and bring to a boil, then slowly whisk in the polenta. Take your time to avoid clumps. Bring back to a boil, then reduce the heat to low and simmer, stirring frequently, for 45 minutes. Stir in the butter. The polenta is ready when it is soft and shiny with the texture of mashed potato.

If you have a pressure cooker, you can reduce the cooking time for the polenta. Set the cooker to sauté setting. Place the stock and salt in the cooker, cover with a lid (not the pressure cooker lid) and bring to a boil. Slowly whisk in the polenta. Add the butter, cover and lock the pressure cooker lid and set to high pressure for 15 minutes. Manually release the pressure and stir the polenta with a wooden spoon until smooth.

About 20 minutes before the polenta is ready, heat the olive oil in a large frying pan over a medium heat, add the onion and sauté for 5 minutes. Add the chili and garlic and stir until the chili has softened, then add the tomato and cook, covered, for about 5 minutes.

Add the shrimp and season with salt and pepper, then cover and simmer for 4 minutes, or until the shrimp are pink and cooked through.

Spoon the polenta onto a large wooden board or serving platter and top with the shrimp and tomato mixture. Finish with a generous sprinkling of cilantro and serve warm.

TIP

The poblano pepper can be replaced with a green bell pepper (capsicum), if preferred.

Mushroom & Apple Polenta
WITH CREAMY PARMESAN SAUCE

It is a rustic Italian tradition to pour hot polenta onto a wooden board to set, then spoon it directly onto serving plates. For a brief time, I sold my Southwestern take on these mesquite polenta boards, a venture that ended up being so successful that I spent weeks in my backyard doing nothing but sanding, sawing and epoxying. Considering I hadn't made anything with wood since my summer camp days, it wasn't one of my best ideas. One month of constant sawdust was enough for me. I replaced my saw with a wooden spoon and headed back into the kitchen to make the actual polenta! This is a warm and comforting dish perfect for chilly fall weather.

Serves 6

1.2 liters (41 fl oz/5 cups) vegetable stock

30 g (1 oz/2 tablespoons) butter

150 g (5½ oz/1 cup) polenta

SAUTÉED MUSHROOM AND APPLE

2 tablespoons olive oil

4 portobello mushrooms, wiped clean and thickly sliced

2 yellow apples, peeled, cored and cut into wedges

1 tablespoon chopped rosemary

½ teaspoon fine sea salt

PARMESAN SAUCE

120 ml (4 fl oz/½ cup) dry white wine

240 ml (8 fl oz/1 cup) vegetable stock

60 g (2 oz/¼ cup) heavy (thick/double) cream

50 g (1¾ oz/½ cup) grated parmesan

Combine the vegetable stock and butter in a large saucepan over a medium heat. Cover and bring to a boil, then slowly whisk in the polenta. Take your time to avoid clumps. Bring back to a boil, then reduce the heat and simmer, stirring frequently, for 45 minutes, or until the polenta is soft and creamy.

If you have a pressure cooker, you can reduce the cooking time for the polenta. Set the cooker to sauté setting. Place the stock and butter in the cooker, cover with a lid (not the pressure cooker lid) and bring to a boil. Slowly whisk in the polenta. Cover and lock the pressure cooker lid and set to high pressure for 12 minutes. Manually release the pressure and stir the polenta with a wooden spoon until smooth. It will continue to thicken as it cools, so set aside for 5 minutes before serving; when it's done the polenta should be soft and creamy but not runny.

Shortly before you are ready to serve, prepare the sautéed mushroom and apple. Heat the olive oil in a frying pan or skillet over a medium heat, add the mushroom and sauté for about 3 minutes until it begins to soften. Add the apple, rosemary and salt and continue to cook until the apple starts to brown and is soft but not mushy. Scoop the mixture into a bowl and set aside. You will be using the pan to make the sauce.

For the sauce, pour the white wine and stock into the pan or skillet and bring to a simmer over a medium heat. Simmer until it has reduced by half, scraping the bottom of the pan with a wooden spoon to deglaze. Remove from the heat and stir in the cream and parmesan until melted and smooth.

To assemble, spoon the polenta onto a large wooden board or serving platter, layer the sautéed mushroom and apple on top and finish with the cream sauce. Serve warm.

Jammy Tomato Cobbler
WITH SOUR CREAM CORNMEAL BISCUITS

While this is not exactly a dessert cobbler, it falls somewhere in between sweet and savory. The fig jam brings out the natural sweetness of the tomatoes and the cornmeal biscuits have just the right amount of saltiness. Whatever you call it, it's completely delicious and a great way to use up a bumper crop of cherry tomatoes.

Serves 6

120 g (4½ oz/1 cup) all-purpose (plain) flour (or use bread flour or whole wheat flour)

140 g (5 oz/1 cup) yellow cornmeal

3 tablespoons granulated sugar

2 teaspoons baking powder

½ teaspoon baking soda (bicarbonate of soda)

¼ teaspoon fine sea salt

115 g (4 oz/½ cup) butter, melted

120 ml (4 fl oz/½ cup) whole (full-cream) milk, plus extra for brushing

115 g (4 oz/½ cup) sour cream, plus extra to serve

115 g (4 oz/1 cup) grated sharp cheddar or gruyere

1 teaspoon chopped rosemary

JAMMY TOMATOES

60 ml (2 fl oz/¼ cup) olive oil

½ red onion, finely sliced

2 garlic cloves, finely chopped

2 teaspoons finely chopped rosemary

540 g (1 lb 3 oz/4 cups) cherry tomatoes

3 tablespoons apple-cider or red-wine vinegar

2 tablespoons fig or apricot jam

½ teaspoon fine sea salt

For the jammy tomatoes, heat the olive oil in a 23 cm (9 in) cast-iron skillet or frying pan over a medium heat, add the onion and sauté for 5 minutes, stirring frequently. Add the garlic, rosemary and cherry tomatoes and cook for 5 minutes, or until the tomatoes start to soften and collapse. Stir in the vinegar, jam and salt, reduce the heat to low and cook for 20 minutes, stirring occasionally. This will allow the juices to reduce and thicken, creating this cobbler's signature jammy texture.

Preheat the oven to 190°C (375°F).

Combine the flour, cornmeal, sugar, baking powder, baking soda and salt in a large mixing bowl. In a separate bowl, mix together the butter, milk and sour cream. Pour the milk mixture into the dry ingredients and combine with a wooden spoon.

Remove the tomatoes from the heat. Using two tablespoons, scoop up a generous portion of dough and gently drop it on the tomatoes. Repeat with the remaining dough, creating an evenly spaced layer of biscuits on top. They will expand as they bake, covering the tomato filling.

Brush the biscuits with extra milk and sprinkle with the cheese and rosemary. Bake for 35 minutes, or until the biscuits are golden. Allow to cool for 10 minutes and serve warm with a dollop of extra sour cream.

Cornmeal Arancini

STUFFED WITH GREEN OLIVES AND GRUYERE

I am a big fan of this underappreciated Sicilian gem. Dainty enough to lay out as a lovely appetizer, yet also filling enough to serve as a main meal, this cornmeal take on stuffed rice balls is great to take to a dinner party. Or to keep all to yourself at home. Either way, the phrase 'just one more' is bound to come up.

Somehow sage always thrives in my garden, no matter how insane the temperatures get during a Phoenix summer. It became necessary to invent this sage pesto, and I actually think it gives the traditional basil version a real run for its money. But of course, if time is short, a store-bought pesto is just fine too.

Makes about 36

480 ml (16 fl oz/2 cups) whole (full-cream) milk

280 g (10 oz/2 cups) yellow cornmeal

1 teaspoon fine sea salt

1 teaspoon sweet paprika

1 tablespoon finely chopped thyme

1 egg

30 g (1 oz/2 tablespoons) butter

30 g (1 oz) gruyere (or Emmental, taleggio or mozzarella)

36 pitted Castelvetrano (Sicilian) olives or other green olives, drained

canola oil, for deep-frying

SAGE PESTO

1 cup sage leaves

1 cup Italian (flat-leaf) parsley leaves

130 g (4½ oz/1 cup) walnuts

120 ml (4 fl oz/½ cup) olive oil

2 garlic cloves, roughly chopped

juice of ½ lemon

½ teaspoon fine sea salt

½ teaspoon freshly ground black pepper

To make the sage pesto, place all the ingredients in a food processor and blend until smooth. Taste and adjust the seasoning if needed. Set aside.

Line a rimmed baking sheet with parchment (baking) paper.

In a medium heavy-based saucepan, bring the milk and 240 ml (8 fl oz/1 cup) water to the boil over a high heat. Slowly add the cornmeal, whisking it so it doesn't form into clumps. Add the salt, paprika and thyme. Reduce the heat to low, add the egg and butter and mix with a wooden spoon until the batter is thick and stiff. Remove from the heat and carefully pour the batter onto the prepared sheet. Cover to prevent it from drying out and set aside to cool.

Meanwhile, cut the cheese into 36 small cubes and stuff a piece inside each olive.

When the cornmeal batter is cool enough to handle, take a piece the size of a ping-pong ball (or 30 g/1 oz, if you want to be precise) and flatten it in the palm of your hand to make a disk. Dip your hands in water if you find the batter too sticky or too dry. Place a stuffed olive in the middle of the disk, then wrap the cornmeal around to completely enclose it and form a ball. Repeat with the remaining batter and olives.

Pour 5 cm (2 in) of canola oil into a large heavy-based saucepan and heat to 175°C (350°F), or until a cube of bread dropped into the oil browns in 15 seconds. Add half the arancini and fry for about 6 minutes until they are golden brown. Remove with a slotted spoon and drain on paper towel. Repeat with the other half.

Serve warm with the sage pesto.

Chorizo Cornmeal Soup

WITH SPINACH AND LIME

This humble, velvety soup is known by different names all over the world, and features particularly in South American cuisine. It's perfect for warming up the bones on a wintry day. Cotija is a dry salty cheese that pairs beautifully with the flavors in this dish. If you can't find it in your area, feta makes a good substitute.

Serves 4

2 tablespoons olive oil

½ onion, finely chopped

2 garlic cloves, finely chopped

225 g (8 oz) ground (minced) pork chorizo

960 ml (32½ fl oz/4 cups) chicken stock

45 g (1½ oz/⅓ cup) fine yellow cornmeal

30 g (1 oz/1 cup packed) chopped spinach

100 g (3½ oz/1 cup) crumbled Cotija cheese, to serve

lime wedges, to serve

Heat the olive oil in a medium heavy-based saucepan over a medium heat and sauté the onion and garlic until they are softened and fragrant. Add the chorizo and cook, breaking up any clumps with your wooden spoon, until browned and cooked through.

Pour in the stock and bring to a boil. Gradually whisk in the cornmeal, then reduce the heat and simmer for 25 minutes, or until the cornmeal has softened and the stock starts to thicken. Add the spinach and cook until wilted. Serve with crumbled Cotija and a squeeze of lime.

TIP

If you are preparing this soup ahead of time, note that the cornmeal will continue to absorb the liquid so you may need to thin it down with a bit more stock before serving.

Nested Eggs in Baked Polenta

WITH GOAT'S CHEESE AND SMOKED TROUT

There are so many different ways to make polenta, but I particularly love this skillet/oven method. It makes the creamiest, plumpest polenta that seems to magically turn into reconstituted corn on the cob. Plus, it only requires stirring once, halfway through cooking. You can serve this dish straight from the skillet, just be sure to warn your brunch guests that the handle is piping hot!

Serves 6

150 g (5½ oz/1 cup) polenta

480 ml (16 fl oz/2 cups) vegetable stock

480 ml (16 fl oz/2 cups) whole (full-cream) milk

2 tablespoons melted butter

½ teaspoon fine sea salt

115 g (4 oz) smoked trout or salmon, bones removed, crumbled

285 g (10 oz) goat's cheese

½ cup packed chopped dill, hard stems removed

1 bunch scallions (spring onions), finely chopped

6 eggs

2 tablespoons capers, rinsed if salt-packed (optional)

lemon wedges, to serve

Preheat the oven to 200°C (400°F).

In a large bowl, mix together the polenta, stock, milk, butter and salt. Pour into a 30 cm (12 in) ovenproof skillet or frying pan, then carefully place in the middle of the oven but without a rack above it (so you can comfortably stir the mixture without having to remove the skillet). Bake for 35–40 minutes, stirring halfway through, until the polenta has softened and thickened and all the liquid has been absorbed.

Take the skillet out of the oven. Stir in the smoked trout or salmon and about two-thirds of the goat's cheese, dill and scallion (save the rest for garnish). Use the back of a large spoon to create six indents in the polenta. Crack an egg into each indent and sprinkle with the remaining goat's cheese.

Heat the oven broiler (grill) to its highest setting. Return the skillet to the oven and bake for another 5–10 minutes until the egg whites are set but the yolks are still a bit runny, and the goat's cheese is bubbly and golden.

Garnish with the remaining dill and scallion and serve with capers, if using, and lemon wedges.

Pink Polenta

WITH CRISPY GARLIC AND PANCETTA

In the early days of the mill, we cleaned all the polenta by hand. This entailed swirling shallow dishes of polenta until the pericarp (the outer layer of the corn that's notorious for getting stuck in everyone's teeth) collected at the top of the bowl, where we'd scoop it off between two palms. It was tedious work, and nearly impossible to get all the pericarp. Over the years, we've hacked together some improvements to the method that allow us to process larger quantities, but none of them have been what you could call efficient. I've agonized over how we can get our polenta as perfectly clean and polished as our commercial competition, but gradually I came to realize that this slightly 'dirty' polenta is actually a good thing – the mark of an artisanal product. So when you're buying polenta, look for speckles of color and flakes of pericarp to know you've got the good stuff.

Serves 6

3 medium red beets with their green tops

960 ml (32½ fl oz/4 cups) chicken stock

1 teaspoon fine sea salt

60 ml (2 fl oz/¼ cup) olive oil, divided

150 g (5½ oz/1 cup) polenta

100 g (3½ oz/1 cup) grated parmesan

115 g (4 oz) pancetta, cut into small cubes

4 garlic cloves, very finely sliced lengthwise

freshly ground black pepper

microgreens, to garnish (optional)

Separate the beets from their tops. Set the greens aside for later. Peel the beets and chop them into 1 cm (½ in) cubes.

Combine the chicken stock, salt, beet cubes and 2 tablespoons of the olive oil in a large saucepan over a medium heat. Cover and bring to a boil, then slowly add the polenta, whisking constantly to avoid any clumps. Bring back to a boil, then reduce the heat and simmer for 45 minutes, stirring frequently, until the beet cubes are soft and the polenta is creamy. Stir in the parmesan until melted through.

If you have a pressure cooker, you can reduce the cooking time for the polenta. Set the cooker to sauté setting. Place the stock, salt, beet cubes and 2 tablespoons of the olive oil in the cooker, cover with a lid (not the pressure cooker lid) and bring to a boil. Slowly whisk in the polenta. Cover and lock the pressure cooker lid and set to high pressure for 15 minutes. Manually release the pressure and stir the polenta with a wooden spoon until smooth. Stir in the parmesan until melted through.

Meanwhile, roughly chop the reserved beet stems and leaves into pieces. Pan-fry the pancetta over a medium heat until the fat renders, then add the garlic and cook for another couple of minutes until the pancetta is crispy and the garlic is lightly browned. Transfer the pancetta and garlic to a plate and set aside.

Heat the remaining 2 tablespoons olive oil in the same pan over a medium heat and sauté the chopped beet greens for 15 minutes, or until dark green and softened. Remove from the heat.

To assemble, spoon the pink polenta onto a platter and top with the beet greens and crispy pancetta and garlic. Finish with a grinding of pepper and some microgreens, if using. Serve hot.

DURUM

Durum wheats warrant some extra up-front explanation as durum is the only wheat that gets a new name after it is milled. We call the flour emerging from the mill either semolina or durum flour, depending on how the flour is milled and sifted.

We'll take semolina first: semolina is the coarse endosperm of the durum and can range in size from granulated sugar to turbinado (raw sugar), depending on what it will be used for. Semolina is usually the sole ingredient in dried extruded pasta. On the other hand, durum flour is the starchy part of the grain – a golden-yellow flour thanks to the high level of beta carotene in durums. Durum flour is typically used to make bread.

To add to the confusion, at our mill we create an additional product that combines a finely ground semolina with our durum flour and call it 'semolina flour'. I found that this mixture gave the most versatile flour for the home kitchen, the best of both worlds. If you can't find a ready-made mixture like our semolina flour, you can mix any fine semolina and durum flour 50/50.

Over the years, we have grown several varieties of heritage durum wheats and landed on Blue Beard Durum as our favorite variety for its flavor and drought tolerance. Our first crop of this durum was grown with Gary John on his farm in Hyder, Arizona. Gary was instrumental in bringing this seed out of the seed bank and into the light of day (his story is told with embellishment in the introduction to Carrot Cavatelli, page 160).

Gary threw that first seed into cracked brown desert earth. With little encouragement, the seed came up and thrived, reaching almost 5 feet tall, with dark blue, plump heads with matching mountain man beards. That first crop tasted sweetly triumphant.

FLAVOR PROFILE

Blue Beard Durum has a soft honey taste with notes of cardamom and fresh-cut pine.

SUBSTITUTES

Another heritage durum to seek out is Durum Iraq, or use conventional durum.

Sweet Roman Gnocchi

WITH WHIPPED HONEY RICOTTA

A few seasons back, our durum farmer called and told us that a huge bag of durum fell off their truck, then they ran over it and it exploded in the road like a giant juicy grape. Not to worry though – the vast majority of the grain was safely stowed and already on its way to the mill. This is just one of the many anecdotes that endear our farmers to us. These wonderful, down-to-earth folks consistently grow some of the most flavorful grains we've ever found. They certainly grow the best Blue Beard Durum in Arizona (though, to be fair, they are also the only ones in the country who grow it). It's as if the grain has not only taken on the terroir of the land, but the sweet disposition of the farmers who grow it.

This is a sugary twist on traditionally savory Roman gnocchi, made with the semolina milled from durum. Crispy on the outside and custardy on the inside, these make for a crowd-pleasing Sunday brunch.

Serves 8–10

715 ml (24 fl oz/3 cups) whole (full-cream) milk

60 g (2 oz/4 tablespoons) unsalted butter

3 tablespoons granulated sugar

½ teaspoon fine sea salt

½ teaspoon freshly grated nutmeg

210 g (7½ oz/1 heaped cup) semolina flour

2 egg yolks

3 tablespoons turbinado or raw sugar

380 g (13½ oz/2 cups) summer berries (raspberries, blueberries, blackberries or strawberries)

WHIPPED HONEY RICOTTA

225 g (8 oz/1 cup) fresh ricotta, well drained

2 tablespoons honey

grated zest of 1 lemon

Preheat the oven to 230°C (450°F). Line a 46 cm × 33 cm (18 in × 13 in) rimmed baking sheet with parchment (baking) paper or a silicone baking mat. Grease a 25 cm (10 in) round baking dish.

Combine the milk, butter, granulated sugar, salt and nutmeg in a heavy-based saucepan over a medium heat and bring to a boil. Keep a close eye on it as it has a tendency to boil over. When it has reached the boil and the butter has melted, reduce the heat to low and very slowly whisk in the semolina flour to avoid getting any clumps. As it thickens, switch to a wooden spoon and continue to stir. As the semolina absorbs the milk it will thicken quickly – a wooden spoon should be able to stand upright. At this point, take the pan off the heat and stir in the egg yolks.

Allow the mixture to cool for about 5 minutes, but no more than 10 minutes as it needs to be malleable for the next step. Pour the mixture onto the prepared baking sheet and place a piece of parchment (baking) paper on top, then press or roll it out to an even thickness of about 5–6 cm (¼ in). If the batter is still too warm to touch place a tea towel over the paper.

Using a 6 cm (2½ in) round cookie cutter, cut the semolina mixture into medallions. Re-roll the scraps and cut a few more medallions. (Alternatively, simply cut it into 7.5 cm/3 in squares.) Arrange the medallions, slightly overlapping, in the prepared baking dish and sprinkle over the turbinado or raw sugar. Bake for 25–30 minutes until golden and caramelized.

Meanwhile, to make the whipped honey ricotta, whisk together all the ingredients until light and fluffy.

Serve the gnocchi medallions warm with fresh berries and a dollop of whipped ricotta.

TIP

If you want to prepare this the night before, arrange the gnocchi medallions in the baking dish, then cover and refrigerate overnight. Sprinkle with the sugar and bake in the morning.

One Thousand Hole Pancakes
MOROCCAN BAGHRIR

When I turned six, I begged my mom to let me have my birthday breakfast from McDonald's instead of something homemade. The McDonald's pancake was my idea of pancake perfection, with its spongy texture, so disturbingly similar to the texture of the Styrofoam container it came in, ready to absorb my generous pour of imitation syrup.

While the food scientists who engineered these pancakes may have been onto something, I prefer my buoyant flapjacks to be a little more natural these days. Although I haven't eaten a McDonald's pancake in decades, my nostalgia for a soft, cushiony pancake with a porous surface for soaking up toppings is fully satisfied in these delicious cakes.

These all–durum flour pancakes come from Morocco and are called baghrir. Durum is the basis for couscous and this desert grain is a regular feature in North African cuisine.

Makes 12

220 g (8 oz/1 cup plus 3 tablespoons) semolina flour

½ teaspoon fine sea salt

½ teaspoon instant dry yeast

TAHINI BUTTER

85 g (3 oz/6 tablespoons) butter, at room temperature

65 g (2¼ oz/4 tablespoons) tahini

3 tablespoons honey

Combine the semolina flour, salt, yeast and 415 ml (14 fl oz/ 1¾ cups) warm water in a blender, stopping occasionally to scrape down the side until the mixture is well combined. Let the batter sit at room temperature for 1 hour – it will bubble and expand until almost doubled in size.

To make the tahini butter, combine all the ingredients in a small saucepan. Set aside.

When the batter has rested, pulse the blender for 1 second to remove the large air bubbles.

Heat a small non-stick frying pan over a medium heat. Pour in 60 ml (2 fl oz/¼ cup) of the batter and swirl the pan to spread it out thinly. (If it doesn't spread easily, thin down the batter with another 2–4 tablespoons water.) Cook for 1 minute, or until thousands of small bubbles appear in the surface and the pancake appears dry. There's no need to cook the other side. Carefully lift with a spatula and transfer to a serving platter, then cover with a tea towel to keep warm. Repeat with the remaining batter to make a stack of 12 pancakes.

Warm the tahini butter over a low heat and serve with the pancakes.

TIP

These pancakes are not sweet so they work just as well with savory ingredients. I love using them to soak up the sauce of a hearty stew or curry.

Golden Glow Cake

WITH BLOOD ORANGES

One of the best things about restarting a historic company is the constant discovery of our own history. Customers send us old flour sacks they found in their parents' attic, metal tokens that used to come as prizes in flour sacks, out-of-print history books, you name it. One customer sent an old recipe card put out by the mill in the 1950s for a golden glow cake. I was struck by the wonderfully eccentric name and absolutely had to recreate it (without the Crisco!). The naturally golden color of the semolina, boosted by a bit of turmeric, gave just the right effect.

Serves 8

185 g (6½ oz/1 cup) semolina flour

1 teaspoon baking powder

½ teaspoon baking soda (bicarbonate of soda)

1 teaspoon ground ginger

1 teaspoon ground cardamom

1 teaspoon ground turmeric

½ teaspoon fine sea salt

3 eggs

100 g (3½ oz/½ cup) granulated sugar

120 ml (4 fl oz/½ cup) olive oil

345 g (12 oz/1½ cups) full-fat plain yogurt (not Greek)

1 teaspoon vanilla extract

grated zest of 1 orange

BLOOD ORANGE TOPPING

3 blood oranges (or navel if blood oranges are unavailable)

100 g (3½ oz/½ cup) granulated sugar

45 g (1½ oz/3 tablespoons) butter

Preheat the oven to 175°C (350°F). Line the base of a 23 cm (9 in) springform cake pan with parchment (baking) paper, then grease the base and side of the pan.

Mix together the semolina flour, baking powder, baking soda, ground spices and salt in a large bowl.

In the bowl of a stand mixer fitted with the paddle attachment beat the eggs and sugar on high speed until pale and fluffy. Add the olive oil, yogurt, vanilla and orange zest and mix well. Slowly add the dry ingredients to the wet mixture, mixing at low speed until just incorporated.

Allow the batter to sit at room temperature while you prepare the orange topping.

Using a sharp knife, remove the rind and pith from the oranges, then cut the oranges into 5–6 mm (¼ in) thick slices. In a small saucepan, stir the sugar and butter over a low heat until melted into a nice thick mixture – it doesn't matter if the sugar hasn't completely dissolved. Pour the warm mixture into the prepared pan and spread it as evenly as possible (the heat of the oven will also help with this so don't worry too much). Arrange the orange slices over the top, then carefully pour in the cake batter.

Bake for 45–50 minutes until golden and a skewer inserted into the center of the cake comes out clean. Allow to cool in the pan for 15 minutes, then very gently invert onto a serving plate while still warm, with the blood orange sitting decoratively on top. Leftovers will keep in an airtight container in the fridge for up to 3 days.

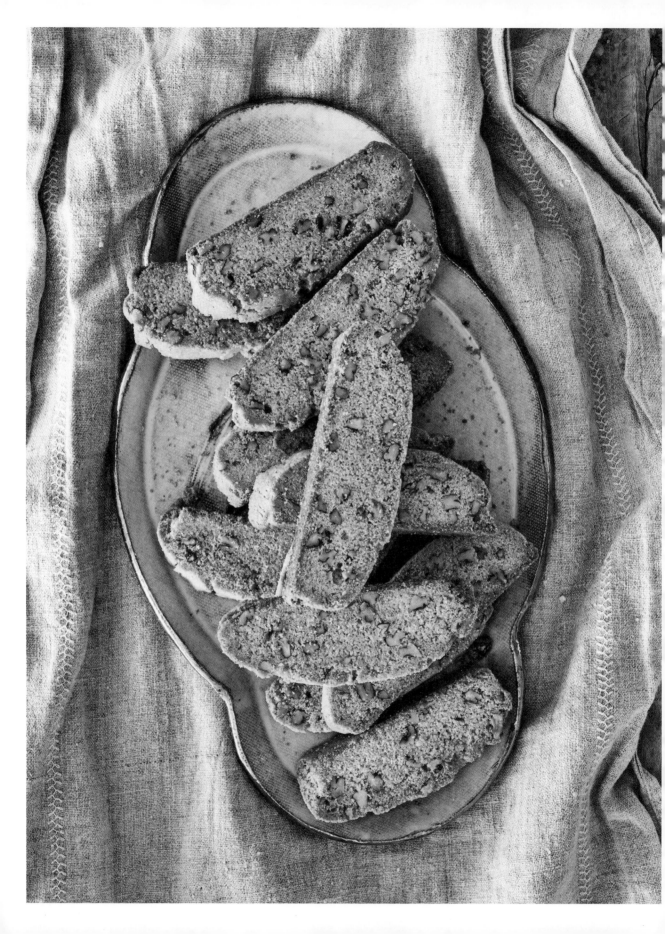

Semolina Biscotti

WITH CORNMEAL AND PECANS

Served with a cup of tea or coffee, I think these toothsome biscotti have just the right level of sweetness. It took a lot of testing and retesting to get the balance right, but my taste-testing husband and siblings finally signed off on this version. In fact, it has been deemed a keeper.

Makes about 24

280 g (10 oz/1½ cups) semolina flour

70 g (2½ oz/½ cup) yellow cornmeal

1½ teaspoons baking powder

¼ teaspoon fine sea salt

120 g (4½ oz/½ cup) unsalted butter, at room temperature

150 g (5½ oz/¾ cup) granulated sugar

2 eggs, at room temperature

1 teaspoon vanilla extract

grated zest of 1 lemon

120 g (4½ oz/1 cup) pecans, finely chopped

Combine the flour, cornmeal, baking powder and salt in a large bowl.

In the bowl of a stand mixer fitted with the paddle attachment, cream the butter and sugar until pale and fluffy. Mix in the eggs one at a time, then add the vanilla and lemon zest. Gradually add the dry ingredients and mix until just incorporated, taking care not to overmix. Finally, mix in the pecans.

Allow the batter to rest at room temperature for 30 minutes or in the fridge for up to 12 hours.

When you are ready to shape the biscotti dough, preheat the oven to 175°C (350°F) and line a baking sheet with parchment (baking) paper.

Divide the dough in half and form into two 13 cm × 7.5 cm (5 in × 3 in) logs. Place on the prepared baking sheet, leaving ample space between the logs as they will spread in the oven. Bake for 30 minutes, or until the tops are lightly golden and starting to crack. Remove from the oven, leaving the oven on, and let them cool for 15 minutes.

Transfer the baked logs to a cutting board and use a serrated knife to cut them into 1 cm (½ in) thick slices. Place the biscotti cut-side up on the baking sheet and bake for 20 minutes, turning halfway through so they become golden on both sides.

Remove and cool completely on a wire rack. The biscotti will keep in an airtight container at room temperature for 4 weeks or in the freezer for up to 3 months.

Window Pane Crackers

WITH MINT AND BASIL

Let me tell you how we came to sell heritage grain crackers. I flew to New York with a suitcase of crackers my dad had made, featuring all the grains we grow. We had managed to secure a meeting with Eataly, one of the biggest specialty food stores in the country. They loved the crackers and ordered a shipment on the spot. I called my dad to share the news, and to ask how we were going to fulfill this order, seeing as this was, you know, a made-up product we didn't manufacture. Was he planning on baking hundreds of crackers in his home oven? In typical fashion, his response was not to worry about the details.

And guess what? We found a great bakery just down the street from the mill. We drop off our freshly stone-milled flours and they turn them into crackers. Although I think the crackers are pretty fantastic (and they've even won some awards), nothing compares to fresh homemade crackers.

Makes 8 large crackers

190 g (6½ oz/1 cup) semolina flour, plus extra for dusting

½ teaspoon fine sea salt

½ cup mint leaves

½ cup basil leaves

olive oil, for brushing

flaky sea salt, to garnish

You'll need a pasta roller to make these crackers.

Combine the flour and salt in a large bowl, then mix in 120 ml (4 fl oz/½ cup) water. The dough will be shaggy and dry at first, but continue mixing until the flour is hydrated and the dough comes together in a ball. Turn out the dough onto a lightly floured work surface and knead for 5 minutes, or until it is smooth and elastic, dusting with a little more flour as needed. Wrap and allow to rest at room temperature for 30 minutes.

Preheat the oven to 200°C (400°F).

Cut the dough into eight pieces. Work with one piece at a time, keeping the rest covered so they don't dry out. Set your pasta roller to the largest setting and feed the dough through. Fold the sheet like an envelope and feed it through the roller once more. Reduce the setting size and feed the dough through once, dusting generously with extra flour as you go to keep it from sticking. Continue rolling, reducing the setting size each time, until the dough is so thin you can see through it – usually the second to last setting of the pasta machine. To check, hold up the sheet: if you can see your hand through it, it's ready.

Lay the mint and basil leaves flat on one half of each dough sheet, then fold the other half on top, as if closing a book. Keeping the pasta roller on the same setting, gently run the dough through the roller to press everything together. Working in batches, place in a single layer on baking sheets, brush with olive oil and lightly sprinkle with flaky sea salt.

Bake for 6–10 minutes (depending on thinness) until the crackers are light brown at the edges and have small bubbles. Keep a close eye on them – they burn easily. Remove and cool on the baking sheets. Repeat with the remaining crackers. Store in an airtight container at room temperature for up to 1 week.

Carrot Cavatelli Pasta

WITH CARROT TOP PESTO

For this recipe you're going to need to allow a little extra prep time. The first step is to visit Monica Spiller, keeper of rare and extinct seeds in California, and ask her to give you a small handful of rare pasta wheat seeds. Plant them in a small plot with care, then keep a close eye on them for seven long months, shooing the birds away from your precious seeds. Once the crop has matured, use a scythe to harvest your small plot. Spread out the wheat heads on a canvas blanket and stomp on them to release the seeds. On a blustery day, get three friends to help man the corners and snap the blanket up in the air so the chaff and straw float away in the breeze. This will leave you with about 45 kg (100 lbs) of clean wheat, assuming you were careful and didn't toss half the seeds into the dirt during an enthusiastic blanket snap. Easy to do, so let's say it's closer to 23 kg (50 lbs). Hang on to it for next year. Repeat for two more years.

While you are waiting for your wheat to grow, retrieve a 50 cm (20 in) round piece of granite and use a chisel to carve uniform furrows in the top face. (Alternately, you could order a ready-to-use mill from Austria and wait patiently for it to round the Magellan passage.)

When you have grown enough seed for at least 10 acres, set about 1800 kg (2 tons) aside for next year's planting. Clean the rest of the seeds for milling. The cleaning method you used before was fine for replanting, but now you need to get it food-grade clean. To achieve this, balance a floor fan on top of a bucket and pour the wheat back and forth between two other buckets until all the tiny little sticks and bits of chaff have blown off. Once that's done, you will be left with only the wheat seeds – oh, and the weed seeds, which are helpfully the same size as the wheat seeds. So, spread out the wheat on a blanket and pick through each individual granule, one by one. To maintain some degree of sanity, don't think of this as a tedious, mind-numbing task, but rather as a sort of Zen meditation. Whatever you do, don't overlook tiny stones, as those can destroy your mill.

And just like that, you are ready to mill. First, soak the wheat in water to bring it up to 15 per cent moisture (you might need to revisit some high school math at this point). When the wheat has fully absorbed all the water and feels completely dry, dump it into the hopper of the mill. Set the millstone close to the mill, but not too close; just barely scraping but not to the point where you smell the burning of granite on granite. Once you've finished this process for your entire crop of wheat, make yourself some pasta. You've earned it.

Serves 6

375 g (13 oz/2 cups) semolina flour, plus extra for dusting

245 g (8½ oz/1 slightly heaped cup) carrot puree (see Tip)

½ teaspoon fine sea salt

CARROT TOP PESTO

green tops from 1 large bunch of carrots, tough stems removed (save the carrots for the pasta)

2 packed cups basil leaves

70 g (2½ oz/½ cup) pepitas (pumpkin seeds)

120 ml (4 fl oz/½ cup) olive oil

100 g (3½ oz/1 cup) grated parmesan

2 garlic cloves, roughly chopped

zest and juice of 1 lemon

½ teaspoon fine sea salt

Place the semolina flour, carrot puree and salt in a large bowl and mix with a wooden spoon until it starts to form a dough. Turn out onto a lightly floured work surface and knead for 5 minutes until the dough is smooth and elastic. Cover with airtight wrap and rest at room temperature for 30 minutes.

Meanwhile, to make the pesto, blend all the ingredients in a food processor or blender until smooth.

Cut the dough into eight pieces and work quickly to roll them into long snakes, about 1 cm (½ in) thick. Cut the snakes into 2.5 cm (1 in) segments. Dust a cavatelli board (also known as a gnocchi board) with flour and hold it at a 45-degree angle, bracing the base against your work surface. Take one piece of dough at a time and, using the pad of your thumb, push it down while at the same time scraping it against the board. The dough will naturally curl in on itself. Repeat with the remaining dough.

Bring a large saucepan of salted water to the boil. Add the cavatelli and cook for 8–12 minutes until al dente. Drain, reserving 120 ml (4 fl oz/½ cup) of the pasta water.

In a large bowl, toss together the pesto, hot pasta and a good splash of the reserved pasta water until emulsified and well coated. Serve immediately.

See step-by-step images on pages 162–63.

TIP

To make the puree, roughly chop the carrots (once you have removed the green tops), boil until soft, then puree until smooth. If your bunch of carrots doesn't make quite enough puree, top it up with a little water to get the correct amount.

TIP
If prickly pear fruit is not a regional
harvest in your area and you can't find
prickly pear syrup, use the same quantity of
pomegranate seeds or raspberries instead.

164

THE MILLER'S DAUGHTER

Prickly Pear–Soaked Semolina Cake

WITH PISTACHIOS

Contrary to popular misinformation, the Sonoran desert is bursting with food. Acorns, mesquite pods, cactus pads and wild chilies are abundant. The fruit of the prickly pear is a majestic crown atop the cactus paddle, with a stunning neon-pink interior. It's a tart fruit with a flavor profile somewhere between kiwi fruit and pomegranate.

Soaking this traditional Middle Eastern cake with prickly pear syrup is my own Southwestern twist.

Serves 12

325 g (11½ oz/1¾ cups) semolina flour

30 g (1 oz/½ cup) unsweetened shredded coconut

½ tablespoon baking powder

½ tablespoon baking soda (bicarbonate of soda)

¼ teaspoon fine sea salt

115 g (4 oz/½ cup) butter, at room temperature

200 g (7 oz/1 cup) granulated sugar

3 eggs, at room temperature

1 teaspoon vanilla extract

grated zest of 1 lemon

2 tablespoons lemon juice

240 ml (8 fl oz/1 cup) whole (full-cream) milk

30 g (1 oz/¼ cup) pistachio kernels

PRICKLY PEAR SYRUP

450 g (1 lb) prickly pears, thorns removed (see Tip)

400 g (14 oz/2 cups) granulated sugar

1 teaspoon citric acid or lemon juice

Before you start making the syrup, put on a pair of gloves. Ideally, the prickly pears have already been de-thorned, but there will inevitably be a few small stickers so it's best to be on the safe side. Cut the prickly pears in half and scoop out the flesh, discarding the skin. Place the fruit in a medium saucepan, add the sugar and 480 ml (16 fl oz/2 cups) water. Bring to a simmer and gently mash the fruit as it softens. Gently simmer over a low heat for 40 minutes, then strain the pulp and seeds through a sieve lined with cheesecloth (muslin) into a bowl. Stir in the citric acid or lemon juice. The result will be a clear, vibrant syrup. Set aside to cool before spooning over the cake.

Preheat the oven to 175°C (350°F). Butter the base and sides of a 33 cm × 23 cm (13 in × 9 in) baking dish or line with parchment (baking) paper.

Place the semolina flour and coconut in a high-speed upright blender and blend to a coarse flour consistency. Add the baking powder, baking soda and salt and blend for a few more seconds to incorporate.

In the bowl of a stand mixer fitted with the paddle attachment, cream the butter and sugar on high speed until pale and fluffy. Add the eggs, one at a time, then mix in the vanilla, lemon zest and lemon juice. Slowly mix in the dry ingredients, then gradually add the milk until it is just incorporated into the batter.

Pour the batter into the prepared dish, spread it out evenly with a spatula and bake for 30 minutes. Cover loosely with tinfoil and bake for another 15 minutes, or until a skewer inserted into the center comes out clean. The foil prevents the cake from getting too brown; we want a lighter cake so the bright pigment of the prickly pear syrup really pops.

Allow the cake to cool in the pan for 10 minutes, then turn it out and cut at an angle to form diamonds. Spoon the syrup evenly over the cake and finish by pressing a pistachio into the middle of each piece. The cake will keep in an airtight container at room temperature for up to 3 days.

CHICKPEAS

A flour made from beans is a bit of an outlier in a book about grains, but let me explain myself: beans are the natural complement to wheat. Wheat takes nutrients out of the soil and chickpeas put nutrients back in the soil. Chickpeas are another crop that is wonderfully adapted to our arid climate, requiring less water to grow. Chickpea flour doesn't act like wheat flour – when it's mixed with water it has the texture of panna cotta – and yet this versatile flour can somehow be turned into delicious pasta, crepes and cake. Originally from the Middle East, chickpeas are one of the earliest cultivated legumes. They are high in protein and an important staple in many cuisines, including Mediterranean, Middle Eastern and Indian. You may feel you know all you need to know about the humble garbanzo bean if you're already a hummus lover, but these recipes explore a more nuanced side of chickpea flavor, putting a surprisingly flavorful spin on dishes you may never have thought would shine with the inclusion of this globally loved legume.

FLAVOR PROFILE

Chickpea flour is warm and buttery with a hint of nutmeg.

SUBSTITUTES

When looking for chickpea flour, also keep an eye out for gram or besan (both commonly used alternative names).

Chickpea Chocolate Chip Cookies

First, grab a sticky note and bookmark this page. Since I began developing material for this cookbook, I have made these cookies at least twenty times, but never with the intention to improve the recipe. In fact, this was the only recipe in this book that came out perfectly the first time!

I am not a proponent of 'healthy' recipes masquerading as substitutes for 'junk food'. I simply believe in real food, and this is some *really* delicious real food, with enough sugar and butter to satisfy any sweet tooth. The tahini and chickpea flour play off each other for a sophisticated take on the classic peanut butter chocolate chip cookie.

Makes 24

210 g (7½ oz/1½ cups) Chickpea Flour

60 g (2 oz/½ cup) all-purpose (plain) flour

½ teaspoon fine sea salt

½ teaspoon baking soda (bicarbonate of soda)

115 g (4 oz/½ cup) butter

325 g (11½ oz/1½ cups) brown sugar

50 g (1¾ oz/¼ cup) granulated sugar

130 g (4½ oz/½ cup) tahini (see Tip)

1 egg

1 teaspoon vanilla extract

170 g (6 oz/1 cup) dark chocolate chips

flaky sea salt, to garnish

Preheat the oven to 175°C (350°F). Line two cookie sheets with parchment (baking) paper.

Combine the flours, salt and baking soda in a large bowl.

In the bowl of a stand mixer fitted with the paddle attachment, cream the butter and sugars on high speed until smooth. Reduce the speed and add the tahini, egg, vanilla and 2 tablespoons water, then mix on high speed until pale and fluffy. Slowly add the dry ingredients and mix on low speed until combined, then gently mix in the chocolate chips.

Scoop out 1 tablespoon balls of dough and space them evenly on the prepared cookie sheets. Chill in the freezer for 5 minutes (to reduce spreading during baking), then bake on the middle rack of the oven for 15 minutes. If the cookies have puffed up in the center, give the cookie sheet a strong tap on the countertop to flatten them. Sprinkle lightly with flaky salt and cool for 10 minutes, then transfer to a wire rack to cool completely. The cookies are best on the day of baking but will keep in an airtight container at room temperature for up to 3 days. As with peanut butter cookies, they become quite firm after day one.

TIP

The tahini should be the consistency of honey – dripping off a spoon but not runny. If your tahini is a little dry, stir in a splash of warm water.

THE MILLER'S DAUGHTER

Rosa Farinata

with RED ONIONS and PISTACHIOS

When we moved our mill into the back of Chris Bianco's restaurant (see page 12), I took the opportunity to snoop around for the *secret ingredient* to his food. Everything I'd eaten from the Bianco kitchen was the best meal I'd ever had; and it's not like I hadn't eaten good food before – I was raised by food lovers. There was just something extraordinary about this food.

Our mill was squeezed in right next to the back door of the restaurant, so I had a clear view of who and what came in and out. It was a revolving door of Phoenix's farmers carrying crates of newly harvested produce, buckets of fresh goat's cheese, and just-butchered lambs over their shoulders. I never once saw a food distributor's semi-truck pulled up to the back door, just real farmers with dirt on their hands and sunglasses tans. So, as I should have guessed, the secret ingredient turned out to be the ingredients themselves and the people who produced them with such care. No snooping required.

This is my homage to my favorite Bianco pizza, the Rosa, in farinata form (an Italian chickpea crepe). The Rosa pizza sustained us through those long days and late nights at the mill, often eaten straight from the box on the back door stoop.

Serves 8 as an appetizer

140 g (5 oz/1 cup) Chickpea Flour

1 teaspoon fine sea salt

1 teaspoon freshly ground black pepper

1–2 tablespoons finely chopped rosemary

60 ml (2 fl oz/¼ cup) olive oil, divided

½ large red onion, finely sliced

30 g (1 oz/¼ cup) raw pistachio kernels, roughly chopped

1 lemon, finely sliced (optional)

100 g (3½ oz/1 cup) finely grated parmesan

Place the chickpea flour, salt, pepper, rosemary, half the olive oil and 240 ml (8 fl oz/1 cup) warm water in a bowl and whisk until there are no visible clumps. (You could also use a blender to mix this together in no time.) Allow the batter to hydrate at room temperature for 30 minutes, or in the fridge for up to 12 hours.

Preheat the oven to 190°C (375°F). Place a 25 cm (10 in) cast-iron skillet or non-stick pizza tray in the oven to heat as it comes to temperature.

Carefully remove the incredibly hot skillet from the oven and coat the base with the remaining olive oil. Pour in the chickpea batter and evenly sprinkle with the red onion, pistachios and lemon slices, if using. Return to the oven and bake for 15 minutes, or until the edges are crisp and brown and starting to pull away from the side of the skillet. Remove from the oven, add the parmesan and bake for another 2 minutes until the cheese is melted and starting to brown.

Remove and cool for 5 minutes, then slice and serve warm.

Chickpea Frites

WITH PRESERVED LEMON MAYO

Move over sweet potatoes – there's a new fry on the block. Although they are slightly less starchy, these chickpea frites are crispy on the outside and custardy on the inside, with a satisfying crunch that makes them feel like a guilty pleasure. You won't regret making these, but you'll certainly regret it when they're all gone.

Serves 8 as an appetizer

2 teaspoons olive oil

280 g (10 oz/2 cups) Chickpea Flour

1 teaspoon fine sea salt

1 teaspoon freshly ground black pepper

safflower oil (or other high-heat oil), for deep-frying

1 bunch Italian (flat-leaf) parsley, leaves picked and finely chopped

½ tablespoon coarse sea salt

PRESERVED LEMON MAYO

115 g (4 oz/½ cup) mayonnaise

2 tablespoons preserved lemon paste

To make the preserved lemon mayo, mix together the mayo and lemon in a small bowl. Set aside.

Cut two pieces of parchment (baking) paper to fit on a 33 cm × 23 cm (13 in × 9 in) rimmed baking sheet and lightly grease them. Place one on the bottom of the baking sheet and set the other one aside.

Combine the olive oil and 960 ml (32½ fl oz/4 cups) water in a large saucepan over a high heat. Just before it boils, slowly add the chickpea flour and whisk to remove any clumps and form a smooth batter. Season with the salt and pepper and reduce the heat to low. Switch to a wooden spoon and cook, stirring constantly, for 10 more minutes, or until the batter thickens and pulls away from the side of the pan.

Scoop the batter onto the greased parchment and spread it out to a 1 cm (½ in) thickness. Work quickly as the batter will start to firm up as it cools. Place the second piece of greased paper on the batter and gently press to smooth it out evenly. Set aside for 30 minutes to allow the batter to cool and set, then cut into sticks, approximately 12 cm × 2.5 cm (4.5 in × 1 in).

Pour 1 cm (½ in) of the safflower oil into a deep heavy-based saucepan and heat to 175°C (350°F). To check, carefully dip one end of a chickpea stick into the oil; if it sizzles, it's ready. Working in batches so you don't overcrowd the pan, gently add the chickpea sticks to the hot oil and cook, turning with tongs when needed, until they are golden on both sides, about 3–5 minutes. Remove and drain on paper towel.

Toss the hot frites in the parsley and coarse salt and serve hot with the preserved lemon mayo.

Inside Out Falafel

CHICKEN SHAWARMA WRAP

I can never decide between shawarma and falafel, but it has dawned on me that I shouldn't have to choose. Together they make an absolutely dynamic combination, and here I've incorporated the grassy, piquant flavors of falafel into a crepe wrap to hold a simple shawarma filling. Sahten!

Makes 6

store-bought or homemade hummus, to serve

1 teaspoon ground sumac

CHICKEN SHAWARMA AND ROASTED TOMATO FILLING

450 g (1 lb) chicken breast fillets

2 tablespoons shawarma spice

juice of 1 lemon

60 ml (2 fl oz/¼ cup) olive oil

150 g (5½ oz/1 cup) cherry tomatoes

FALAFEL CREPES

140 g (5 oz/1 cup) Chickpea Flour

½ teaspoon cumin seeds

½ teaspoon fine sea salt

2 packed cups mixed chopped greens (scallion/spring onion, flat-leaf/Italian parsley, cilantro/coriander or mint)

olive oil, for brushing

CUCUMBER YOGURT

230 g (8 oz/1 cup) Greek yogurt

3 garlic cloves, finely chopped

½ teaspoon fine sea salt

1 Persian cucumber (cuke), seeds scraped, grated

To make the filling, place the chicken breasts, shawarma spice, lemon juice and olive oil in a large bowl and toss to coat the chicken. Set aside to marinate in the fridge for at least 1 hour or up to 12 hours.

Preheat the oven to 220°C (425°F). Place the chicken and cherry tomatoes on a rimmed baking sheet and roast for 40 minutes, or until the chicken is golden and cooked through and the tomatoes are bubbly and juicy. Just before serving, finely slice the chicken.

Meanwhile, for the falafel crepes, combine the chickpea flour, cumin seeds, salt, most of the greens (reserve a little for garnish) and 300 ml (10 fl oz/1¼ cups) water in a blender and mix on high to form a smooth batter. Brush a 23 cm (9 in) frying pan or crepe pan with a little olive oil. Heat over a medium heat, pour in 60 ml (2 fl oz/¼ cup) of batter and swirl the pan to spread it evenly over the base. Cook for about 1 minute until bubbles form, then flip and cook for another minute. Transfer the crepe to a plate and repeat with the remaining batter to make six crepes in total, brushing with extra oil as needed.

To prepare the cucumber yogurt sauce, combine all the ingredients in a small bowl.

To assemble, spread hummus over the falafel crepes and top with sliced chicken and roasted tomatoes and some of the cucumber yogurt. Garnish with the reserved herbs and dash of sumac, then roll up and serve.

Chickpea Lasagna

WITH HERBED RICOTTA AND RED PEPPER SAUCE

You know I can't let you charge into a recipe without fair warning: this one has project status! But the results are totally worth it – a comforting vegetarian lasagna featuring red pepper sauce rather than tomato, and a cross-cultural inspiration for a hearty chickpea noodle.

Serves 6

2 small zucchini (courgettes), cut into 3 mm (⅛ in) thick medallions

2 small eggplants (aubergines), peeled and cut into 3 mm (⅛ in) thick medallions

PASTA DOUGH

245 g (8½ oz/1¾ cups) Chickpea Flour, plus extra for dusting

2 eggs

1 tablespoon olive oil

½ teaspoon fine sea salt

RED PEPPER SAUCE

3 tablespoons olive oil

1 onion, finely chopped

3 garlic cloves, finely chopped

1 teaspoon fine sea salt

1 tablespoon dried oregano

2 × 340 g (12 oz) jars roasted red peppers, including the liquid

HERBED RICOTTA

450 g (1 lb) fresh ricotta, drained

450 g (1 lb) feta

1 egg

1 bunch Italian (flat-leaf) parsley, leaves picked and finely chopped

Start by making the pasta dough. It will need time to rest and fully hydrate and during this time you can prepare the other ingredients.

Place the chickpea flour on a large wooden board in a mound and make a well in the middle. Add the eggs, olive oil, salt and 1 tablespoon warm water to the well, then use a fork to break up the eggs and then slowly incorporate the flour into the well to make a slurry. Keep adding the flour until the mixture forms a shaggy dough, then knead for about 5 minutes until it comes together in a smooth ball. Cover the dough with airtight wrap and allow to rest at room temperature for at least 30 minutes, or in the fridge overnight.

Meanwhile, prepare the red pepper sauce. Heat the olive oil in a heavy-based saucepan over a medium heat and sauté the onion until soft and translucent, about 5 minutes. Add the garlic, salt, oregano and roasted peppers and their liquid. Reduce the heat to low and simmer for 20 minutes. Remove from the heat and cool slightly, then use a stick blender, upright blender or food processor to puree the mixture into a sauce. Don't make it too smooth – it should still have a bit of texture. Set aside.

For the herbed ricotta, place all the ingredients in a large mixing bowl and mix with a fork. Set aside.

When the dough has rested, get out your pasta machine and divide the dough into four pieces. Work with one piece at a time and keep the remaining dough covered so it doesn't dry out. Each piece should make enough rolled pasta for one layer of the lasagna.

Set your pasta roller to the largest setting and feed the dough through. Fold the sheet like an envelope, dust with flour and feed it through the roller several more times. Reduce the setting size and feed the dough through once, dusting with extra flour as you go to keep it from sticking. Don't fold it this time. Continue rolling, reducing the setting size each time, until the dough is 2 mm (1/16 in) thick (about the thickness of three playing cards). Don't worry too much about getting precise rectangles – melted cheese will cover up any little imperfections.

Cut the sheets into 33 cm (13 in) lengths, or to fit your baking dish. Mine is 33 cm × 23 cm (13 in × 9 in).

Preheat the oven to 190°C (375°F).

You are now ready to assemble the lasagna. Spread a small amount of red pepper sauce over the base of your baking dish to prevent the noodles from sticking. Start layering in this order: lasagna noodles, red pepper sauce, zucchini and eggplant slices, ricotta mixture. Continue layering this way with the remaining ingredients, finishing with the last of the ricotta mixture.

Cover with tinfoil and bake for 45 minutes. Remove the foil and bake for another 20 minutes, or until the cheese is nicely browned on top. Take the lasagna out of the oven and let it sit for 15 minutes before cutting and serving.

CHICKPEAS

Curry Cauliflower Pakoras

Over the 10,000 years that the chickpea has been domesticated, South Asian culture has really refined its milling and use to a fine art, and I highly recommend seeking out authentic Indian recipes for inspiring ways to use chickpea flour. Pakoras, for example, are simply vegetables coated in chickpea flour and fried. This is a handy recipe to have in your repertoire as just about any type of vegetable can be used.

Chickpeas are a semi-arid crop, meaning they require less water than crops that developed in more temperate climates, so they grow well in Arizona. As a bonus, legumes add nitrogen back into the soil, so they are a great rotation crop for maintaining healthy fields. Chickpeas grow on petite bushes close to the ground, and each chickpea emerges from a single green pod.

Serves 6 as an appetizer

175 g (6 oz/1¼ cups) Chickpea Flour

35 g (1¼ oz/¼ cup) rice flour

1 tablespoon curry powder

1 teaspoon ground cumin

½ teaspoon cayenne pepper

½ teaspoon ground ginger

½ teaspoon garlic powder

½ teaspoon fine sea salt

½ teaspoon baking powder

1 head cauliflower, cut into bite-sized florets

canola oil (or other high-heat oil), for deep-frying

MINT YOGURT SAUCE

230 g (8 oz/1 cup) Greek yogurt

juice of 1 lime

2 tablespoons finely chopped mint

pinch of fine sea salt

Combine the flours, curry powder, spices, salt and baking powder in a large bowl. Slowly mix in 175 ml (6 fl oz/¾ cup) water to form a smooth batter. If the batter is clumpy, let it rest for a few minutes, giving the chickpea flour a bit more time to absorb the water, then stir it again. Dip the cauliflower florets in the batter to coat, allowing the excess to drip back into the bowl.

Pour 5 cm (2 in) of canola oil into a large heavy-based saucepan and heat to 175°C (350°F), or until a cube of bread dropped into the oil browns in 15 seconds. Working in batches so you don't overcrowd the pan, deep-fry the battered cauliflower for 3 minutes each side, or until puffed and golden. Remove with a slotted spoon and drain on paper towel.

To make the mint yogurt sauce, combine all the ingredients in a small bowl. Serve with the warm pakoras.

TIP

To make kimchi fritters, drain off the excess liquid from 400 g (14 oz) mild kimchi and finely chop. Make the chickpea batter as above, add the kimchi and mix well to combine. Heat the oil. Use a cookie scoop to form tablespoons of battered kimchi into balls and drop it into the oil. Flatten the balls into fritters with the back of a wooden spoon and fry for 2–3 minutes each side, or until puffed and golden. Drain and serve warm.

Chickpea Flour Pound Cake

WITH TAHINI GLAZE

It seems that whenever I'm pregnant, I have very intense dreams about food, specifically cakes and bagels. The idea for this cake came to me in one of these dreams and the next morning I couldn't decide if it was pure genius or more akin to pickle-flavored ice cream. I researched my idea and discovered that there is a traditional Mexican cake made of whole chickpeas. Genius, then? Anyway, it gave me the confidence to develop this recipe. The Middle Eastern spice mix baharat adds warmth to the cake and makes for a particularly fragrant day of baking. The tahini glaze rounds out this lightly sweetened cake, making it suitable for breakfast or dessert. Serve with mint tea.

Serves 8

160 g (5½ oz/1 cup) White Sonora Type 00 Flour

160 g (5½ oz/1 cup + 2 tablespoons) Chickpea Flour

1 teaspoon baking powder

½ teaspoon fine sea salt

2 teaspoons baharat spice mix

225 g (8 oz/1 cup) unsalted butter, at room temperature

300 g (10½ oz/1½ cups) granulated sugar

3 eggs

2 teaspoons vanilla extract

120 ml (4 fl oz/½ cup) buttermilk

TAHINI GLAZE

230 g (8 oz/2 cups) powdered (icing) sugar

130 g (4½ oz/½ cup) tahini

GARNISHES

edible flowers (optional)

powdered (icing) sugar

Preheat the oven to 175°C (350°F). Grease or line a 23 cm × 13 cm (9 in × 5 in) loaf (bar) pan with parchment (baking) paper, leaving a 5 cm (2 in) overhang on each long side to help lift the cake out easily.

Combine the flours, baking powder, salt and spice mix in a medium bowl.

In the bowl of a stand mixer fitted with the paddle attachment, cream the butter and sugar until light and fluffy. Add the eggs one at a time and mix to incorporate, then stir in the vanilla. Gradually add the flour mixture and the buttermilk and mix until well combined.

Transfer the batter to the prepared pan and smooth the surface. Place on the middle rack of the oven and bake for 1 hour, or until golden and a skewer inserted in the center comes out clean. A little batter sticking will be fine as the cake will continue to bake as it cools. Remove the cake from the oven and cool for about 15 minutes, then lift it out of the pan and cool to room temperature.

To make the tahini glaze, combine the sugar and tahini in a small bowl. Gradually blend in enough hot water to thin the mixture to a glazing consistency – this could be anything from 3–6 tablespoons.

Place the cooled cake on a wire rack set over a baking sheet and spread the tahini glaze over the top, allowing the excess to drip down the sides. Garnish with powdered sugar and edible flowers, if using. Cut into slices and serve. Store leftover cake in an airtight container at room temperature for up to 3 days.

OATS

I still remember a phone call from my dad, very early one morning, and he was so excited he could barely get the words out: 'I'm standing in Brent's oat field and you have to taste these oats!' I could clearly picture him in the field, threshing oats in his hand, popping them in his mouth and talking with his mouth full. 'They taste like butter! Is this what oats are supposed to taste like?' I've never known anyone to get this worked up about oats, ever. We generally hear of people 'choking down' a bowl of gluey oatmeal in the morning for the health benefits. Oats are one of the most ubiquitous grains that I explore in this book, but the oats that get us excited, the ones that smell like oatmeal cookies straight from the field, are still quite hard to source. They are raw oats. The thing that makes fresh oats so delicious is their high oil content, but it also makes them susceptible to going rancid, something that does not go over well with the industrial food system. The moment an oat goes through a roller, its oils are exposed to the air and the clock starts ticking on its pretty short expiration date. This is why most conventional rolled oats have been heat-treated or steamed to neutralize the oils, which is a real shame because so much flavor is lost as a result. These days, it might even be easier to find heritage grains than raw oats that haven't been heat-treated.

At Hayden Flour Mills, we decided to sell whole oat groats because they are most stable in that form. Oats are a very soft grain, so they're easy to turn into flour or cracked oats in a home blender. We also make cracked oats, and we seal these after removing the oxygen to delay the oxidation process. For freshly rolled oats, we sell a home oat roller. There are only two recipes for rolled oats in this chapter (Salty Seedy Granola on page 184 and Basic Oatmeal on page 202) because, even though they are the easiest mentioned in here to find at your local supermarket, they are the hardest to find fresh. I do wish you the best of luck in finding fresh oats near you though, because once you've tasted them you won't want to go back. The best way to preserve any oat product is to store it in the freezer.

FLAVOR PROFILE

Simply put, freshly milled oats taste like oatmeal cookies, with notes of cinnamon and brown butter and faintly tannic undertones.

Salty Seedy Granola

WITH MISO AND APRICOTS

I like my granola extra salty, but there is a limit to how much you can add to granola before you ruin it. The miso might seem like a surprising ingredient here, but it adds a crave-worthy depth to the flavor, without being overpowering.

Serves 8

300 g (10½ oz/2 cups) rolled (porridge) oats

40 g (1½ oz/1 cup) puffed brown rice (or puffed quinoa)

2 tablespoons sesame seeds

30 g (1 oz/¼ cup) sunflower seeds

60 g (2 oz/½ cup) roughly chopped pecans or cashews

60 ml (2 fl oz/¼ cup) melted coconut oil or olive oil

2 tablespoons yellow miso paste

60 ml (2 fl oz/¼ cup) maple syrup

2 tablespoons brown sugar

½ teaspoon fine sea salt

100 g (3½ oz/½ cup) dried apricots, chopped into small pieces

Preheat the oven to 150°C (300°F). Line a rimmed baking sheet with parchment (baking) paper.

Combine the oats, puffed rice, seeds and nuts in a large mixing bowl.

In a saucepan over a low heat, stir the oil, miso paste, maple syrup, brown sugar and salt until the miso has dissolved, without letting the mixture come to a boil. Once the sauce is smooth, pour it over the oat mixture and stir everything together.

Transfer the granola to the prepared baking sheet and spread it out evenly. Bake for about 40 minutes, turning the tray halfway through for even cooking. Watch closely towards the end as it can quickly go from toasted and golden to downright burnt. Pull it out as it turns golden as it will continue to crisp as it cools. Mix in the dried apricot and allow it to cool completely. The granola will keep in an airtight container for up to 1 week.

Vegan Bone Broth

By extracting the natural oils from the oats, this grain broth can simulate the rich, fatty mouthfeel that is so loved in traditional bone broths. If you have some saved vegetable scraps on hand, such as leek greens and carrot peels, by all means use those instead of the whole vegetables called for in the recipe. Broths are a great way to preserve nutrients and cut down on kitchen waste. This rich broth is delicious sipped on its own or used as the base for a vegan stew, or any stew, for that matter.

Makes about 2 liters (68 fl oz)

170 g (6 oz/1 cup) Oat Groats

1 leek, well washed, with green tops

6 large button mushrooms, halved

½ teaspoon black peppercorns

½ tablespoon fine sea salt

3 garlic cloves, roughly chopped

6 carrots, roughly chopped

Toast the oat groats in a large stockpot over a medium heat for 3 minutes, stirring with a wooden spoon so they don't catch and burn. Add the remaining ingredients and 2 liters (68 fl oz) water and bring to a boil, then reduce the heat and simmer, uncovered, for 1½ hours. Strain the broth through a fine sieve and discard or compost the solids.

If you have a pressure cooker, you can reduce the cooking time for this recipe. Set the cooker to sauté, add the oat groats and toast for 3 minutes, stirring with a wooden spoon so they don't catch and burn. Add the remaining ingredients and 2 liters (68 fl oz) water, cover and lock the lid, then set to high pressure for 40 minutes. Manually release the pressure, then strain the broth, discarding or composting the solids.

The broth will keep in the fridge for 5 days, or freeze for up to 3 months.

Superfood Oatmeal Smoothie

I could really just call this a 'chocolate shake for breakfast' because that's what it tastes like to me! It's a great all-in-one breakfast smoothie, combining your morning cup of coffee with your morning bowl of oats, boosted with omega-3 rich superfoods like hemp, chia and flax seeds. It's perfect for days when you have a long to-do list to tackle and need to keep moving. Most of the prep should be done the night before so the oat mixture has time for a good soak, then it all comes together in minutes in the morning.

Serves 2

50 g (1¾ oz/⅓ cup) Cracked Oats or rolled (porridge) oats

3–4 pitted dates, to taste

30 g (1 oz/¼ cup) unsalted cashews

1 tablespoon hulled hemp seeds

1 teaspoon chia seeds

1 teaspoon flax seeds (linseeds)

pinch of fine sea salt

1 frozen overripe banana

2 shots of espresso or strong iced coffee (see Tip)

1 cup ice cubes

Combine the oats, dates, cashews, seeds and salt in a heatproof bowl and pour over 240 ml (8 fl oz/1 cup) boiling water. Give it a quick stir, then cover and leave to soak at room temperature overnight.

In the morning, place the soaked mixture in a blender, add the frozen banana, coffee and ice and blend on high speed until smooth and creamy.

TIP

If you are not a coffee drinker, replace with 1 teaspoon matcha powder.

Cacio E Pepe Ris-oat-o

WITH CRISPY SHALLOTS

My dad likes to call me up and open with, 'Do you want to hear a funny story?' Now, 'funny story' is code for 'something terrible has happened but don't worry, I've already found the silver lining'. They can range from 'we've just lost our biggest customer' to 'our oats have gone rancid and taste terrible!' *Oh great,* I think, *rancid oats. A marketing nightmare.* But here's Dad, right on the ball with a bright side: 'Isn't that incredible? It proves our theory that it's the oils that make fresh oats so delicious you can eat them straight from the field. If oats can go bad, it means that they really are meant to be eaten fresh!' And he's right; this is a fantastic revelation. The significance of what we've observed carries us forward in our commitment to fresh oats. We recover from the loss, and I can see the value in the lesson provided by nature. But you still won't catch me laughing at his 'funny stories'.

Based on the famous pasta dish cacio e pepe, this is the easiest risotto you will ever make. And if you are able to get your hands on fresh-from-the field oats, it will also be the most delicious risotto you will ever make.

Serves 4

30 g (1 oz/2 tablespoons) butter

½ onion, finely chopped

4 garlic cloves, finely chopped

150 g (5½ oz/1 cup) Cracked Oats

120 ml (4 fl oz/½ cup) dry white wine

480 ml (16 fl oz/2 cups) vegetable or chicken stock

150 g (5½ oz/1½ cups) finely grated parmesan

freshly ground black pepper

fresh basil, to garnish (optional)

CRISPY SHALLOTS

4 shallots, finely sliced into rounds

60 ml (2 fl oz/¼ cup) olive oil

½ teaspoon flaky sea salt

To make the crispy shallots, place the shallot in a small frying pan, cover with the olive oil and cook, stirring occasionally, over a medium heat for 20 minutes until golden brown. Keep a close eye on the pan as they can burn quickly. Remove with tongs and drain on paper towel, then toss with the flaky salt and set aside.

Melt the butter in a medium saucepan over a medium heat, add the onion and garlic and sauté for 5 minutes, or until fragrant and translucent. Add the oats and sauté for 2 minutes until lightly toasted. Pour in the white wine and let the oats absorb the liquid, then add the stock. Bring to a boil, then reduce the heat and simmer for 15–20 minutes, stirring frequently, until the liquid has been absorbed and the oats are soft with a bite. Stir in the parmesan and eight grinds of the pepper mill.

Serve the risotto warm topped with crispy shallots. Garnish with basil, if using.

If you would rather use a pressure cooker to make the risotto, set the cooker to sauté and melt the butter in the pot while it heats up. Add the onion and garlic and sauté for 5 minutes, or until fragrant and translucent. Add the oats and sauté for 3 minutes until lightly toasted. Pour in the white wine and let the oats absorb the liquid, then add the stock. Turn off the sauté setting, cover and lock the lid and set to high pressure for 5 minutes. Allow the pressure cooker to naturally release the pressure for 10 minutes. Remove the lid and stir in the parmesan and eight grinds of the pepper mill.

Vegan Bolognese

This is a vegan riff on Marcella Hazan's perfect bolognese sauce. A chef friend once told me that the best way to add whole canned tomatoes to a sauce is to crush each one in your fist. Give it a try if you don't mind getting your hands dirty.

Serves 6

60 ml (2 fl oz/¼ cup) olive oil

½ onion, chopped

150 g (5½ oz/1 cup) finely chopped carrot

100 g (3½ oz/1 cup) finely chopped celery

240 ml (8 fl oz/1 cup) dry white wine

1 × 800 g (1 lb 12 oz) can peeled plum tomatoes with juices

2 teaspoons fine sea salt

freshly ground black pepper

½ teaspoon garlic powder

½ tablespoon brown sugar

150 g (5½ oz/1 cup) Cracked Oats

240 ml (8 fl oz/1 cup) almond milk

450 g (1 lb) pasta (fettucine or spaghetti)

chopped Italian (flat-leaf) parsley, to garnish (optional)

VEGAN PARMESAN

30 g (1 oz/¼ cup) whole unsalted cashews

2 tablespoons nutritional yeast

¼ teaspoon garlic powder

pinch of fine sea salt

Heat the olive oil in a sauté pan over a medium heat and sauté the onion until fragrant and translucent. Add the carrot and celery and cook for another 5 minutes, then pour in the wine and simmer until it has evaporated. Add the canned tomatoes and their juices, crushing them by hand or with a wooden spoon, then add the salt, pepper, garlic powder and brown sugar. Simmer, uncovered, for 2 hours to allow the flavors to really meld together. Keep an eye on it, stirring and adding a good splash of water if the sauce becomes too thick and starts to burn on the bottom.

Add the oats and 240 ml (8 fl oz/1 cup) water and simmer for another 30 minutes, or until the oats have softened but still have enough bite to mimic the mouthfeel of ground beef. Stir in the almond milk and simmer for 5 minutes.

To make the vegan parmesan, pulse all the ingredients in a food processor until coarsely crumbled, with a similar texture to grated parmesan.

Cook the pasta in a large saucepan of salted water according to the packet instructions. Drain, reserving about 120 ml (4 fl oz/ ½ cup) of the pasta water. Add the pasta to the sauce and stir to coat, mixing in the reserved pasta water if the sauce is a little thick.

Serve generously garnished with vegan parmesan, some extra black pepper to taste, and parsley, if using.

If you have a pressure cooker, you can reduce the cooking time for this recipe. Set the cooker to sauté. When it comes to temperature, add the oil and onion and sauté until fragrant and translucent. Add the carrot and celery and cook for another 5 minutes, then pour in the wine and simmer until it has evaporated. Add the canned tomatoes and their juices, crushing them by hand or with a wooden spoon, then add the salt, pepper, garlic powder and brown sugar. Cover and lock the lid, then set to high pressure for 20 minutes. Manually release the pressure and add the oats, then cover and lock the lid again and set to manual for 5 minutes. Manually release the pressure and keep on the warm setting. Add the almond milk. If the sauce isn't thick enough, return to sauté setting and simmer until reduced and thickened to the desired consistency.

Toasted Oatmeal Pies

WITH ORANGE AND GINGER CREAM CHEESE FILLING

Just as it does with nuts, toasting grains really brings out a whole new level of flavor. The best trick is to go by smell: when the oat flour starts to smell like popcorn, take it off the heat. This toasted oatmeal method makes a very solid oatmeal cookie if you're not up for turning them into pies.

Makes 22

300 g (10½ oz/2½ cups) oat flour (see page 48)

115 g (4 oz/½ cup) unsalted butter, at room temperature

110 g (4 oz/½ cup) dark brown sugar

70 g (2½ oz/⅓ cup) granulated sugar

1 egg

1 teaspoon vanilla extract

½ teaspoon baking soda (bicarbonate of soda)

½ teaspoon fine sea salt

½ teaspoon ground cinnamon

½ teaspoon ground ginger

¼ teaspoon freshly grated nutmeg

CREAM CHEESE FILLING

170 g (6 oz) cream cheese, at room temperature

115 g (4 oz/½ cup) butter, at room temperature

255 g (9 oz/2¼ cups) powdered (icing) sugar

2 tablespoons orange juice

¼ teaspoon ground ginger

¼ teaspoon fine sea salt

Preheat the oven to 175°C (350°F). Line two cookie sheets with parchment (baking) paper or silicone baking mats.

Heat a cast-iron skillet or non-stick frying pan over a medium heat, add the oat flour and toast, stirring regularly, for 3–5 minutes. Keep a close eye on it as the flour can burn easily. It's done when the flour just begins to turn golden and smells deliciously like popcorn. Transfer the flour to a plate or bowl and set aside to cool.

In the bowl of a stand mixer fitted with the paddle attachment, cream the butter and sugars on high speed until combined. Add the egg and vanilla and mix until pale and fluffy.

Combine the toasted oat flour, baking soda, salt, cinnamon, ginger and nutmeg in a bowl. Add to the butter mixture and mix on low speed until incorporated.

It's not advisable to let this batter rest for too long before baking as the oat flour absorbs the ambient moisture, creating a thicker cookie.

Form the cookie dough into 44 balls (30 g/1 oz each) and place on the prepared cookie sheets, leaving plenty of room for spreading. I find it helpful to weigh the dough as it ensures the cookies are an even size, something you will thank yourself for when you sandwich them with the cream filling. Bake the cookies for 8–10 minutes until they are golden around the edge and still slightly soft in the center. When you take each cookie sheet out of the oven, bang it on the counter to flatten the cookies. Cool slightly, then transfer to a wire rack and leave to cool completely.

While the cookies are cooling, make the cream filling. In the bowl of a stand mixer fitted with the paddle attachment, cream together the cream cheese, butter and sugar until fluffy. Mix in the orange juice, ginger and salt.

To assemble the pies, scoop a heaped tablespoon of cream filling onto the base of a cookie and gently press another cookie on top, like a sandwich. Repeat with the remaining cookies and filling. The filled cookies will keep in the fridge for up to 3 days. If you don't think they will all be eaten within a day or two of baking, the unfilled cookies and filling can be stored separately in the fridge for up to 1 week, ready for assembly when the craving strikes.

Overnight Oat Bake

WITH CHERRIES AND ALMONDS

This recipe doubles as an instruction manual for becoming a morning
person – that rare breed that wakes before light in a state of perfect
cheerfulness. Enjoying the morning doesn't come naturally to me, but with
three kids, early wake-up calls are part of the gig. I find that prepping
breakfast the night before helps me look forward to the mornings.

You could also make this with rolled oats, but I love the heartier texture
the cracked oats bring to the dish.

Serves 8

375 g (13 oz/2½ cups) Cracked
Oats or rolled (porridge) oats

1 tablespoon flax (lin) seeds
(optional)

1 tablespoon chia seeds
(optional)

1 × 400 ml (13½ fl oz) can coconut
milk

2 eggs

80 ml (2½ fl oz/⅓ cup) maple
syrup, plus extra to serve

70 g (2½ oz/⅓ cup) dark brown
sugar

60 ml (2 fl oz/4 tablespoons)
melted unsalted butter

2 teaspoons baking powder

1 teaspoon vanilla extract

1 teaspoon almond extract

½ teaspoon fine sea salt

285 g (10 oz) frozen or fresh
pitted cherries

60 g (2 oz/½ cup) slivered
almonds

cream, to serve

Grease a 20 cm (8 in) square baking pan.

Place all the ingredients, except the cherries, slivered almonds
and cream, in a large bowl and mix thoroughly. Pour the
mixture into the prepared pan and smooth the surface, then
cover and refrigerate overnight (this will allow the oats to
hydrate and soften).

In the morning, preheat the oven to 175°C (350°F).

Decorate the top of the oat mixture with the cherries and
almonds, then bake for 45–50 minutes until the edges start to
brown and the middle is just set. The baking time will affect the
final texture so bake a little longer for a firmer result, and for
a shorter time if you prefer a more pudding-like consistency.

Cut into squares (or any shape you like) and serve warm with
cream and a drizzle of extra maple syrup.

Retro Oatflour Pancakes

WITH COTTAGE CHEESE AND PEANUT BUTTER

These are an update on a family classic. The recipe came to me from my mother-in-law, torn out of an old spiral-bound cookbook from an era when it was in vogue for entire cookbooks to feature cottage cheese and vats of homemade yogurt. These pancakes are the last word in comfort food for my husband's whole family. We make a double batch most Saturday mornings and the kids eat them as they come off the griddle. The thin batter makes them ideal for pouring into the shape of a certain famous cartoon mouse, which never fails to delight the little ones (and sometimes the grown-ups, too).

Makes about 24 small pancakes

60 g (2 oz/½ cup) oat flour (see page 48)

4 eggs

225 g (8 oz/1 cup) cottage cheese

½ teaspoon fine sea salt

1 teaspoon vanilla extract

60 ml (2 fl oz/¼ cup) melted coconut oil

3 tablespoons natural peanut butter

120 ml (4 fl oz/½ cup) milk (or milk alternative)

strawberry jam and powdered (icing) sugar, to serve (optional)

Place all the ingredients, except the jam and powdered sugar, in a blender and blend on high speed until smooth. The batter should be thin like a crepe batter, resulting in a thin pancake with a soft, cheesy center.

Heat a small skillet or griddle (hotplate) over a medium heat and pour in about 3 tablespoons of batter per pancake. Cook for 1 minute, or until small bubbles begin to form, then flip and cook for another minute. Serve warm with strawberry jam and a dusting of powdered sugar, or any other topping you like.

TIP

If you make the batter the night before, the oat flour will absorb some of the liquid, so thin the batter with 2–4 tablespoons milk before cooking.

Savory Steamed Pumpkin Porridge

WITH MISO OATS AND SESAME

This Japanese-inspired dish is a savory porridge pairing salty oatmeal and sweet pumpkin. I feel nourished just thinking about it. It's easy to whip up in a rice cooker with a steamer basket, making for a hands-off all-in-one meal. If you don't have the equipment, simply cook the oats and steam the squash separately.

Serves 4

150 g (5½ oz/1 cup) Cracked Oats

1–2 tablespoons yellow miso paste (depending on how salty you want it)

½ Kabocha squash (Japanese pumpkin), skin and seeds removed, cut into 2.5 cm (1 in) thick wedges (see Tip)

1 tablespoon brown sugar

1 tablespoon sesame oil or olive oil

4 eggs

8 small radishes, finely sliced

1 bunch chives or scallions (spring onions), finely sliced

1 tablespoon sesame seeds (white or black)

chili oil or chili crisp, to serve (optional)

Place the cracked oats in a rice cooker, cover with 600 ml (20½ fl oz/2½ cups) water and stir in the miso paste – it will dissolve completely as it cooks.

Toss together the squash, brown sugar and oil in a bowl, then layer the squash in the rice cooker's steamer basket. The brown sugar will enhance the caramelization of the squash as it steams. Place the basket on top of the cooker and cover, then set to 'cook'. It should take about 15 minutes.

Shortly before the oats and squash are ready, fry the eggs until the whites are set but the yolks are still runny.

Divide the porridge between four bowls. Top with the steamed pumpkin and egg (or serve the egg on the side), garnish with the radish, chives and sesame seeds and serve warm with chili oil or chili crisp, if you like.

TIP

If you can't source a Kabocha squash, any other sweet squash variety will work here. Red kuri is particularly good.

Oatmeal Cookie Milk

Although it can (and should) be made from nothing more than oats and water, store-bought oat milk often has a long list of unfamiliar ingredients, so it's worth whipping up a homemade batch if you can. The steps in this recipe are designed to keep the milk from developing too much starch, which results in a texture that can only be described as 'slimy' and not what I'd call pleasant to drink. Trust me. You really need to follow the steps.

Serves 6

40 g (1½ oz/⅓ cup) unsalted cashews

85 g (3 oz/½ cup) Oat Groats (see Tips)

3 pitted Medjool dates

½ teaspoon ground cinnamon

½ teaspoon vanilla extract

pinch of fine sea salt

Soak the cashews in water for 30 minutes to soften. They will add a nice creaminess to the oat milk.

Toast the oat groats in a frying pan over a medium heat for 5 minutes until fragrant and lightly golden. Transfer the oats to a bowl and set aside.

Drain the cashews and place in a blender. Add the dates and 960 ml (32½ fl oz/4 cups) water and blend on high speed for 1 minute. Add the toasted oat groats, cinnamon, vanilla and salt and blend on high speed for 10 seconds only – this is important. If you blend for any longer the oat milk will start to get starchy and develop that slimy texture I was talking about.

Gently strain the milk through a nut milk bag or clean tea towel into a bottle or pitcher, reserving the pulp (see Tip). Store the milk in the fridge for up to 4 days. It will separate as it sits and this is fine; just give it a quick shake before serving – it foams up beautifully for a latte.

TIPS

An oat groat is the whole oat kernel.

Don't waste the cashew and oat pulp once you've strained the milk. Store it in the fridge or freezer and use it as a high-fiber addition to smoothies.

Cheddar Oat Cakes

Traditional Scottish oatcakes have a sweet-salty balance that pairs well with a slice of sharp cheddar, so here I've taken the liberty of putting the cheese right into the cake (though there is nothing to stop you adding another slice on top). It's worth seeking out European-style butter as its high fat content makes these biscuits just that much better.

Makes about 24

135 g (5 oz/1 heaped cup) oat flour (see page 48), plus extra for dusting

40 g (1½ oz/¼ cup) Cracked Oats or rolled (porridge) oats

60 g (2 oz/4 tablespoons) European-style salted butter, at room temperature

200 g (7 oz) sharp cheddar, grated

4 pitted dates, chopped into small pieces

Preheat the oven to 175°C (350°F). Line a cookie sheet with parchment (baking) paper.

In a large bowl, mix together all the ingredients with a wooden spoon to form a rough dough. Turn out the dough onto a work surface and bring together in a ball, adding a small amount of oat flour if the dough is too sticky. Sandwich the dough between two pieces of parchment (baking) paper and use a rolling pin to roll it out to a 3 mm (⅛ in) thickness.

Use a 4 cm (1½ in) round cookie cutter (or any shape you like) to cut out the cookies, then carefully transfer with a spatula to the prepared cookie sheet. Bake for 15–20 minutes until they are just starting to brown.

Remove and cool completely on the sheet, then store in an airtight container at room temperature for up to 1 week.

Basic Oatmeal

One of our failed side ventures was a scheme to install countertop oat flakers for health food stores; we pictured them sitting companionably beside those grind-your-own peanut butter machines. There really is a night and day difference between the luxe flavor of freshly flaked oats and the staleness of pre-packaged ones, but the tools needed to flake oats at home make it cost-prohibitive for most folks. I really hope someone reading this steals our store flaker idea and runs with it, because, as you can see, we always seem to have more ideas than we know what to do with.

This makes a very simple bowl of oatmeal, but it means you can go all out on the toppings. I've included two of our favorites here to get you started.

Serves 4

150 g (5½ oz/1 cup) Cracked Oats or freshly rolled oats

960 ml (32½ fl oz/4 cups) water or your choice of milk

your choice of topping, to serve (see opposite page)

Toast the oats in a medium saucepan over a low heat for 5 minutes, or until fragrant. Add the water or milk, then increase the heat and bring to a boil, stirring constantly. Reduce the heat and simmer for 25–30 minutes until softened to your desired texture. Serve with your favorite toppings.

Cacao Sprinkles

While I love the deep, slightly bitter taste of cacao nibs, they do need to be used sparingly. The mix is just right here, balanced out by the nuts and coconut. In fact, I find myself sprinkling this over much more than just oatmeal: vanilla ice cream is a particular favorite.

Makes about 280 g (10 oz/2½ cups)

50 g (1¾ oz/⅓ cup) raw pistachio kernels

50 g (1¾ oz/⅓ cup) raw hazelnuts

50 g (1¾ oz/⅓ cup) raw almonds

40 g (1½ oz/⅔ cup) unsweetened coconut flakes

40 g (1½ oz/⅔ cup) cacao nibs

3 tablespoons brown sugar

½ teaspoon ground cinnamon

pinch of fine sea salt

Preheat the oven to 175°C (350°F).

Spread the nuts and coconut flakes evenly over a rimmed baking sheet and toast in the oven for 5 minutes. Remove and cool completely, then place in a food processor with the cacao nibs, sugar, cinnamon and salt and pulse to a coarse crumb. Place in an airtight jar and store for up to 1 month. Sprinkle 1–2 tablespoons over your bowl of oatmeal.

Mo's Magic Mix

Mo is our nickname for my mom, who has a gift for adorning daily staples with simple elements to supercharge their nutrition. This is her technique for upgrading a bowl of morning oatmeal. Feel free to modify the mix to suit whatever nuts, seeds and dried fruit you have on hand.

Makes about 525 g (1 lb 3 oz/3½ cups)

75 g (2¾ oz/½ cup) dried cherries

75 g (2¾ oz/½ cup) slivered almonds

65 g (2¼ oz/½ cup) walnuts, chopped

120 g (4½ oz/½ cup) pitted dates, chopped

40 g (1½ oz oz/⅓ cup) flax seeds (linseeds)

50 g (1¾ oz/⅓ cup) flax meal

30 g (1 oz/¼ cup) hemp hearts

30 g (1 oz/¼ cup) sunflower seeds

40 g (1½ oz/¼ cup) chia seeds

Place all the ingredients in a large airtight jar and shake to combine. Store for up to 1 month. Sprinkle 1–2 tablespoons over your bowl of oatmeal.

RYE

Rye is a figurative late bloomer among the grains. While closely related to wheat and barley, it was long considered an undesirable weed and often shunned for what was considered its bitter taste. It was the food of peasants, or it was fed to animals. Originally native to Turkey and the Levant, it was first cultivated around 13,000 years ago. Over time, rye migrated north, with some archeological evidence pointing to its existence along the Rhine and Danube rivers during Roman times, before it found its place in Russia, Germany, Poland, Latvia, Lithuania and Scandinavia, where it is still beloved today.

Rye is a hardy grain that can tolerate drought and less fertile soils, and is higher in fiber and lower in gluten than its wheat cousin. It has an intense flavor that may take some time to grow on the uninitiated. Rye flour features in many local traditional bread specialties from Europe, such as German pumpernickel. And while it's long been used to make rye whiskey and some beers, it has more recently seen a revival in the world of sourdough baking, as well. Deeply colored and uniquely aromatic, this underdog of a grain really does deserve its time in the limelight.

FLAVOR PROFILE

Rye has the most complex flavor. It reminds me of black coffee in its mood and layered flavors. It's a strange comparison, but it has the slightest taste of fresh hay, and a heady sage and floral aroma when freshly milled.

SUBSTITUTES

Heritage ryes to look for are Gazelle Rye and Wrens Abruzzi Rye, or use a conventional rye.

Sunken Quince Cake

WITH HONEY AND RYE

Quinces are knobbly pome fruits with the texture of an apple and the scent of a guava. The combination of quince, rye flour and honey is a match made in heaven, as this luscious recipe amply demonstrates. The batter rises up over the fruit to create a fun 'sunken' effect that makes this simple tea cake feel fancier than it really is. If quinces are hard to find or out of season, baking apples make a great substitute.

Serves 8

3 quinces

juice of 1 lemon

2 tablespoons granulated sugar

BATTER

150 g (5½ oz/10 tablespoons) unsalted butter, at room temperature

85 g (3 oz/¼ cup) honey

100 g (3½ oz/½ cup) granulated sugar

3 eggs

1 teaspoon vanilla extract

grated zest of 1 lemon

175 g (6 oz/1¼ cups) Rye Flour

2 teaspoons baking powder

¼ teaspoon fine sea salt

100 ml (3½ fl oz) whole (full-cream) milk

powdered (icing) sugar, to serve

Preheat the oven to 175°C (350°F). Butter a 23 cm (9 in) springform cake pan.

Peel the quinces, taking care as some varieties can be very hard, and cut them into halves. Use a tablespoon to scoop out the seeds and tough interior. Score the outside of each piece in 5–6 mm (¼ in) thick slices, being careful not to cut all the way through. As the quince bakes, it will fan apart and the scoring will help to soften the fruit. Toss the prepared quince in the lemon juice and sugar and set aside.

For the batter, in the bowl of a stand mixer fitted with the paddle attachment, cream together the butter, honey and sugar, then add the eggs, one at a time, and beat on high speed until fluffy. Add the vanilla and lemon zest.

Combine the flour, baking powder and salt in a separate bowl, then gradually add to the butter mixture, mixing gently on the lowest speed until incorporated. Mix in the milk.

Pour the batter into the prepared pan and smooth the surface. Arrange the scored quince halves on top, scored side up (if there is room, place the sixth piece in the middle of the cake). There's no need to press them into the batter as the cake will rise around them in the oven.

Bake for 40 minutes until the top of the cake is golden and the quince pieces are soft. Allow the cake to cool completely in the pan, then sift powdered sugar over the top and serve. The cake is best eaten on the day of baking, but leftovers will keep in an airtight container at room temperature for up to 3 days.

Rye Christmas Shortbread

WITH EGGNOG GLAZE

I married into a family that takes Christmas and Christmas cookies
very seriously. My Grinchy heart has thawed over the years and I have
come to love the annual cookie gathering with my in-laws. Springerle
are traditional anise-flavored German cookies that are pressed into
intricate wooden molds. I love collecting reproduction molds and they
work as an easy way to decorate gingerbread or other spiced cookies –
no piping bags required.

Makes 24

280 g (10 oz/2 cups) Rye Flour,
plus extra for dusting

½ teaspoon fine sea salt

1 teaspoon ground ginger

1 teaspoon ground cinnamon

¼ teaspoon freshly grated
nutmeg

¼ teaspoon ground cloves

⅛ teaspoon ground allspice

240 g (8½ oz/1 cup +
1 tablespoon) unsalted butter,
at room temperature

90 g (3 oz/¾ cup) powdered
(icing) sugar

1 teaspoon vanilla extract

EGGNOG GLAZE

3 tablespoons eggnog

145 g (5 oz/1¼ cups) powdered
(icing) sugar

Combine the flour, salt and spices in a medium bowl.

In the bowl of a stand mixer fitted with the paddle attachment,
cream the butter and sugar until light and fluffy. Add the vanilla,
then the flour mixture and mix until a dough forms. Gently
press the dough into a disk, wrap in airtight wrap and rest in
the fridge for at least 30 minutes.

Line two cookie sheets with parchment (baking) paper.

Place the chilled dough on a lightly floured work surface and
roll it out to a 5–6 mm (¼ in) thickness. If it is too cold and
difficult to roll, let it soften slightly at room temperature for
a few minutes.

If you are using a springerle mold, lightly dust the dough and
mold with flour, then press the mold firmly into the dough.
Carefully remove the mold, then, using a thin-bladed knife,
pizza cutter or a slightly larger cookie cutter, cut around the
impression. (The cookies in the photo are 6 cm/2½ in rounds.)
Gently lift the cookie with an offset spatula and place on one of
the prepared cookie sheets. Repeat with the remaining dough,
rerolling the scraps as needed, spacing the cookies about
2.5 cm (1 in) apart. Place the cookie sheets in the freezer for
at least 20 minutes prior to baking. This will help maintain the
impression from the mold.

If you are using regular cookie cutters, cut out any shape you
like and place the cookies on the cookie sheets, as above.
There is no need to put these plain cookies in the freezer.

Preheat the oven to 175°C (350°F).

Bake the cookies for 7–10 minutes (depending on their size)
until fragrant and lightly golden. Remove from the oven and
allow the cookies to cool completely on the sheets.

While the cookies are cooling, mix together the glaze
ingredients in a small bowl. Dip the tops of the cookies into
the glaze and set them back on the sheets for 5 minutes,
or until the glaze has set.

Store in an airtight container at room temperature for up
to 3 weeks.

Carrot Cake Rye Porridge

Rye is a truly beautiful grain. It has a blue-green tinged narrow berry and smells like cacao and walnuts. We grow our rye in partnership with a farmer a few hours north of the mill, taking advantage of the significantly cooler climate that allows the rye to thrive.

Cracking rye in the blender creates a familiar porridge texture in this almost-dessert breakfast dish.

Serves 6

160 g (5½ oz/1 cup) Rye Berries

120 g (4½ oz/1 cup) shredded carrot (about 3 carrots)

80 g (2¾ oz/½ cup) golden raisins (sultanas)

30 g (1 oz/¼ cup) pecans, coarsely crushed

60 ml (2 fl oz/¼ cup) maple syrup

½ teaspoon vanilla extract

½ teaspoon ground cinnamon

¼ teaspoon ground cloves

¼ teaspoon ground ginger

¼ teaspoon freshly grated nutmeg

pinch of fine sea salt

cream, to serve

Put the rye berries in a high-speed blender and pulse for 30 seconds, or until coarsely chopped. The rye might become slightly floury and this is fine: it will make the porridge nice and creamy.

Combine the chopped rye, carrot, raisins, pecans, maple syrup, vanilla, ground spices and salt in a large saucepan, add 960 ml (32½ fl oz/4 cups) water and bring to a boil. Reduce the heat to low and simmer, stirring occasionally, for 40–45 minutes until the porridge is soft. You may need to add an additional 240–480 ml (8–16 fl oz/1–2 cups) water, depending on the coarseness of your chopped rye.

Spoon into bowls and serve with a drizzle of cream.

Chocolate Rye Bourbon Cookies

WITH SEA SALT

I'm trying to make chocolate, bourbon and rye the next great trio:
Athos, Porthos and Aramis. Ron, Harry and Hermione. Blossom, Bubbles
and Buttercup. Chocolate, Bourbon and Rye. I'm telling you. It's gonna
be a classic.

Makes about 24

115 g (4 oz) dark or bittersweet chocolate, chopped

115 g (4 oz/½ cup) unsalted butter, chopped

140 g (5 oz/1 cup) Rye Flour

40 g (1½ oz/½ cup) unsweetened dark cocoa powder

½ teaspoon baking powder

2 teaspoons espresso powder

215 g (7½ oz/1 cup) light brown sugar

200 g (7 oz/1 cup) granulated sugar

¼ teaspoon fine sea salt

2 eggs

1 teaspoon vanilla extract

2 tablespoons bourbon (see Tip)

255 g (9 oz/1½ cups) semisweet or dark chocolate chips

flaky sea salt, for sprinkling

Preheat the oven to 175°C (350°F). Line two cookie sheets with parchment (baking) paper or silicone baking mats. Set aside.

Place the chopped chocolate and butter in a microwave-safe bowl and heat slowly in 10-second increments, stirring until melted and combined. (You could also do this in a heatproof bowl over a saucepan of simmering water.) Set aside in a warm place until needed.

Whisk together the flour, cocoa powder, baking powder and espresso powder in a medium bowl.

In the bowl of a stand mixer fitted with the paddle attachment, mix together the sugars, salt, eggs, vanilla and bourbon. Stop the mixer, add the melted chocolate and butter and stir until thoroughly combined. Add the flour mixture and mix on low speed until incorporated. Fold in the chocolate chips by hand, scraping the bottom of the bowl to make sure all the ingredients are combined. The cookie dough will appear very soft. Let it sit at room temperature for about 10 minutes, or in the fridge for 5–8 minutes if the temperature is quite warm.

Scoop heaped tablespoons of the dough onto the prepared cookie sheets, leaving about 5 cm (2 in) between each one to allow for spreading. Sprinkle a pinch of sea salt over each cookie.

Bake in the middle of the oven for 10–12 minutes until just set in the middle. They will still be quite soft but will firm up as they cool. It's important not to overcook them. Remove the cookies from the oven and cool for at least 30 minutes before transferring to a wire rack to cool completely. Store in an airtight container at room temperature for up to 3 days.

TIP

If bourbon is not to your liking, you can replace it with the same quantity of brewed coffee.

Saffron Strawberry Galette

WITH MESSY RYE CRUST

I have many food memories from my early twenties, when I was learning to cook and traveling often, unafraid to try new things. There's a magic in discovering food when you feel a strong sense of wonder about the world!

This recipe is in memory of Jennifer Gordon, who served me mussels in a saffron white-wine sauce with a green salad garnished with nasturtiums, long before I knew how to appreciate such things. She was a fabulous blend of Scottish roots and the Caribbean island where she grew up, and I was in awe of her bohemian sophistication. Every time I use saffron, I think of her and thank her for including an awkward 24-year-old at her table. Here I use it in a sweet application. If you don't like the scent of saffron you can just leave it out. The galette will still be delicious.

Serves 8

100 g (3½ oz/½ cup) granulated sugar

pinch of saffron threads

450 g (1 lb) strawberries, hulled and sliced

1 teaspoon vanilla extract

1 egg, lightly beaten

2 tablespoons turbinado or raw sugar

CREAM CHEESE PASTRY

225 g (8 oz/1 cup) butter, at room temperature

225 g (8 oz) cream cheese, at room temperature

½ teaspoon fine sea salt

280 g (10 oz/2 cups) Rye Flour, plus extra for dusting

SAFFRON CREAM

pinch of saffron threads

240 g (8 oz/1 cup) heavy (thick/double) cream, plus 2 tablespoons extra

2 tablespoons granulated sugar

To make the pastry, in a stand mixer fitted with the paddle attachment, combine the butter, cream cheese and salt on medium speed until light and fluffy. Slowly add the rye flour, mixing on low speed until the dough comes together in a shaggy ball. Turn out the dough onto a lightly floured work surface and knead into a smooth ball. Form the dough into a disk and wrap in airtight wrap, then rest in the fridge for 30 minutes. (You can also freeze it for up to 3 months.)

While the dough is chilling, use a mortar and pestle or spice grinder to grind the sugar and saffron together. Place in a large bowl, add the strawberries and vanilla and mix together well.

Preheat the oven to 200°C (400°F).

Remove the dough from the fridge and sandwich it between two pieces of parchment (baking) paper. This will stop the rolling pin sticking to the dough and make it easy to transfer it to a baking sheet. Roll the dough into a circle about 35 cm (14 in) in diameter (it doesn't have to be precise). Pile the strawberries in the middle, leaving a 5 cm (2 in) border around the edge. Fold the excess dough over the strawberries, pleating as you go, leaving the fruit in the center exposed. Carefully transfer the galette to a rimmed baking sheet (this is important as you want to catch any strawberry juices that run out). Brush the pastry edges with egg and sprinkle with sugar.

Place the galette on the middle rack of the oven and bake for 30–40 minutes until the crust is a deep golden brown.

Meanwhile, to make the saffron cream, in a small microwave-safe bowl combine the saffron with 2 tablespoons of the heavy cream and microwave for 15 seconds. Set aside to infuse for 15 minutes, then whip with the sugar and remaining cream. Store in the fridge until needed.

Serve warm slices of galette with dollops of the golden cream.

Roasted Sweet Potato Rye Berry Salad

WITH WHISKEY-SOAKED RAISINS

This salad is the perfect addition to a summer barbecue. Fire up the grill, cook some grass-fed hamburgers or steaks, and this tangy salad will single-handedly complete your table.

Serves 8–10 as a side

160 g (5½ oz/1 cup) Rye Berries

50 g (1¾ oz/⅓ cup) golden raisins (sultanas)

1 tablespoon rye whiskey

8 slices of bacon

1 large sweet potato (about 450 g/1 lb), cut into 2.5 cm (1 in) cubes

2 tablespoons olive oil

1 teaspoon cayenne pepper

65 g (2¼ oz/½ cup) walnuts, roughly chopped

140 g (5 oz) blue cheese, crumbled

handful of arugula (rocket) leaves

DRESSING

60 ml (2 fl oz/¼ cup) olive oil

1 tablespoon grainy mustard

½ tablespoon maple syrup

1 tablespoon champagne vinegar or white-wine vinegar

pinch of fine sea salt

Preheat the oven to 220°C (425°F).

Place the rye berries in a large saucepan and cover with 960 ml (32½ fl oz/4 cups) water. Bring to a boil, then reduce the heat and simmer for 1 hour, or until the berries are soft and chewy. Drain and allow to cool.

You can also cook the rye berries in a pressure cooker. Cover the berries with 960 ml (32½ fl oz/4 cups) water and set the cooker to high pressure for 30 minutes. Manually release the pressure, drain and set aside to cool.

Meanwhile, combine the raisins, whiskey and 1 tablespoon boiling water in a small bowl and set aside to soak.

Line two baking sheets with parchment (baking) paper. Place the bacon slices on one sheet. In a large bowl, toss the sweet potato with the olive oil and cayenne, then spread evenly over the second sheet, making sure none of the potato pieces are overlapping. Place both baking sheets in the oven and roast for 30–40 minutes until the bacon is crispy and the sweet potato is soft and starting to brown. Keep an eye on the bacon as it may take less time than the sweet potato. Remove from the oven. When the bacon is cool enough, crumble it into small pieces.

To make the dressing, whisk together all the ingredients.

Combine the rye berries, sweet potato, bacon, raisins (and soaking liquid), walnuts, cheese and arugula in a large bowl. Toss through the dressing and serve.

Rye Gougeres

WITH CARAWAY

When I got married I asked my mom to make me a cookbook of all the family favorites. My one stipulation was that I wanted the originals of these well-worn recipes so I could preserve the physical copies actually used by my mom, berry stains, oil splatters and all. This scrappily assembled cookbook, bound together in a soft leather binder, is one of my most prized possessions. It holds pages pulled from classic resources like the Moosewood cookbooks, *The Silver Palate Cookbook* and wrinkled pages of *Saveur* magazine from a time before quick-search internet recipes. It contains casserole, brownie and pie recipes torn out of a cookbook or magazine, or written on flowery recipe cards with headers like 'From the kitchen of ...' and 'Made with love by ...'. I treasure them, and I keep making them.

One traditional Zimmerman favorite from this collection is gougeres from an old out-of-print French baking book. Required at any festive gathering between Thanksgiving and New Year, this is a heritage grain update on the family classic.

Makes about 20

240 ml (8 fl oz/1 cup) whole (full-cream) milk

115 g (4 oz/½ cup) butter

1 teaspoon fine sea salt

140 g (5 oz/1 cup) Rye Flour

2 teaspoons caraway seeds

½ teaspoon mustard powder

½ teaspoon garlic powder

5 eggs, divided

120 g (4½ oz/1½ cups) grated Emmental (or Swiss) cheese

50 g (1¾ oz/½ cup) grated parmesan

Preheat the oven to 175°C (350°F). Line a baking sheet with parchment (baking) paper.

Combine the milk, butter and salt in a heavy-based saucepan over a medium heat and bring to a boil. As soon as the butter has melted and the mixture begins to boil, remove the pan from the heat and stir in the flour, caraway seeds, mustard powder and garlic powder with a wooden spoon. Return the pan to a low heat and cook for another 5 minutes, or until the dough thickens and pulls away from the side of the pan.

Take the pan off the heat and add four of the eggs, one at a time. Adding the eggs individually is the key to beautifully puffed gougeres, so take your time to incorporate each egg before adding the next. Finally, stir in the Emmental cheese, allowing it to melt.

For each gougere, scoop 1 generous tablespoon of dough onto the prepared sheet. Leave ample space between the gougeres as they will puff up as they bake.

Lightly beat the remaining egg in a small bowl, then brush over each gougere and sprinkle with the grated parmesan.

Bake for 15–20 minutes until the gougeres are puffed, the tops are shiny and the parmesan is lightly golden. Serve warm. These are best eaten on the day of baking.

Seedy Rye Loaf Bread

DANISH RUGBRØD

This style of dense seeded bread is traditionally made with sourdough
starter. Because most of us don't always have a starter on hand, I offer this
modified version which uses pickle juice to replicate the tangy flavor of the
sourdough. I have to say, it's a pretty good forgery, and it lasts for a long
time if stored in airtight wrap. And even when the bread has become too
dry for toast, it lives on as excellent crackers. It's meant to be finely sliced
and used as a base for open-faced sandwiches, such as Reuben, egg salad or
smoked salmon.

I should warn you that, even though this bread doesn't require a sourdough
culture, it is still a bit of a process, involving an initial ferment, two rises
and an overnight wait before you can cut into it. But you will be rewarded
with a flavorful, long-lasting loaf. For a traditional look, this bread is
baked in a Pullman pan, which is a long narrow loaf pan with square sides.

Serves 10

120 g (4½ oz/¾ cup) Rye Berries

100 g (3½ oz/½ cup) White Sonora
Wheat Berries or soft white wheat

350 g (12½ oz/2½ cups) Rye
Flour, divided

120 g (4½ oz/1 cup) flax seeds
(linseeds)

120 g (4½ oz/1 cup) sunflower
seeds

¼ teaspoon instant dry yeast

240 ml (8 fl oz/1 cup) dark beer

240 ml (8 fl oz/1 cup) brine from
lacto-fermented pickles (see Tip)

1 tablespoon malt syrup (or dark
syrup)

240 g (8½ oz/2 cups) all-purpose
(plain) flour

TIP

If you don't have pickle brine,
substitute 240 ml (8 fl oz/1 cup)
buttermilk. When you add the
flours to the fermented mixture,
add 1 tablespoon fine sea salt.

Pulse the rye and White Sonora berries in a blender or food
processor to coarsely break them up (or smash them in a
heavy-duty bag with a meat mallet or other heavy object).

Scoop them into a large bowl. Measure out 100 g (3½ oz) of the
rye flour and add to the bowl, along with the flax and sunflower
seeds, yeast, beer, brine, malt syrup and 480 ml (16 fl oz/2 cups)
water. Stir well, then cover and leave to soak and ferment at
room temperature for at least 8 hours.

After soaking, add the all-purpose flour and remaining rye flour
and stir to combine. Mix by hand for a few minutes (or use a stand
mixer fitted with the dough hook) to form a loose, sticky dough.
Transfer the dough to a large bowl, cover and leave to rise at room
temperature for about 1½ hours until doubled in size.

Grease and flour a 33 cm × 10 cm × 10 cm (13 in × 4 in × 4 in)
Pullman loaf (bar) pan.

At this point, the dough will have a consistency that's closer to
a batter. With the help of a spatula, pour it into the pan, then
tamp it down on the counter to remove any air bubbles. Cover
with a tea towel and leave at room temperature for 1–2 hours
until the dough has expanded to completely fill the pan.

Preheat the oven to 180°C (360°F).

Poke the dough several times with a cake tester or skewer. This
will allow the steam to escape and keep the loaf reasonably
dense. Bake for about 1 hour until it has an internal temperature
of 96°C (205°F) and the top is deeply golden and nicely set.

Tip the loaf out of the pan onto a wire rack. It takes several
hours for the moisture in the loaf to equalize so it's best to wait
until the next day before slicing the bread.

FLOUR & GRAIN RESOURCES

Every regional mill has its own terminology and way of milling, and even different names for the same grains. Small American revival mills have taken inspiration from European traditions, and flour names often end up being a mix of German, French and Italian terminology.

For many years, I compared our Hayden Flour Mills products to an imaginary gold standard, and I drove myself crazy searching for the perfect way to mill our grain. I visited mills in Italy, Lebanon, Canada and all across the US, but what I learned is that every mill does things a little differently. And this is OK! I now feel sure the very best way to mill our grain is just to do it our way: with our values, our regional character, even our limitations, and in the way that tastes best to us.

When our first Austrian stone mill arrived with its slim German manual, it was up to us to figure it out. We milled, tasted what we'd made, and tried again. One of our first customers was a chef from Italy, so we picked up Italian terms like 'Type 00' for our finely ground flour, and we called our coarsely milled corn 'Polenta' instead of 'Grits'. We were like the grain we were attempting to revive – paying attention to our roots, slowly developing our own identity, and drawing from the circumstances, environment and influences around us to grow into our own full flavor as a mill.

The evolution of our product line was heavily influenced by our climate and geography. We don't grow buckwheat or spelt, as those do much better in a cold, wet climate. We chose to focus on reviving grains that originate from arid climates, such as durums and the White Sonoran Wheat, which get its name from our very own Sonoran Desert. You will find that, depending on where you live, your neighborhood mill might do things differently to us. I suppose that's to be expected and celebrated when the whole point of revitalizing regional grains is to counteract the homogeneity of industrial milling.

Listed on the next page are mills from around the world where you will find grains, flours, corn and legumes milled with care. Some are mill-bakeries and mill-farms. Most use stone mills, some are strictly organic. Some focus on heritage varieties and some use conventional wheat varieties but partner with regional farmers to fortify the local food system. All come highly recommended.

UNITED STATES

Anson Mills
ansonmills.com
Columbia, SC

Barton Springs Mill
bartonspringsmill.com
Dripping Springs, TX

Bellegarde
bellegardebakery.com
New Orleans, LA

Blue Bird Grain Farms
bluebirdgrainfarms.com
Winthrop, WA

Camas Country Mill
camascountrymill.com
Eugene, OR

Carolina Ground
carolinaground.com
Asheville, NC

Dry Storage
drystorageco.com
Boulder, CO

Fairhaven Mill
fairhavenmill.com
Burlington, WA

Farm & Sparrow
farmandsparrow.com
Mars Hill, NC

Farmer Ground
farmergroundflour.com
Trumansburg, NY

Grist & Toll
gristandtoll.com
Los Angeles, CA

Honoré Farm & Mill
honoremill.org
Marin County, CA

Janie's Mill
janiesmill.com
Ashkum, IL

Maine Grains
Mainegrains.com
Skowhegan, ME

Marsh Hen Mill
marshhenmill.com
Edisto Island, SC

Meadow Lark Organic
meadowlarkorganics.com
Ridgeway, WI

Mile High Mill
milehighmill.com
Ravendale, CA

Native Seed Search
nativeseeds.org
Tucson, AZ

Ramona Farms
ramonafarms.com
Sacaton, AZ

Shagbark Seed & Mill
shagbarkmill.com
Athens, OH

Sunrise Flour Mill
sunriseflourmill.com
North Branch, MN

Timeless Natural Foods
timelessfood.com
Ulm, MT

Wild Hive Farm
wildhivefarm.com
Clinton Corners, NY

CANADA

Flourist
flourist.com
Vancouver, BC

Moulin de Cèdres
moulindecedres.com
Les Cèdres, QC

AUSTRALIA

Artisan Grains Australia
artisangrainsaustralia.com
Forbes, NSW

Burrum Biodynamics
burrumbiodynamics.com.au
Wimmera, Vic.

Demeter Farm Mill
demeterfarmmill.com.au
Gunnedah, NSW

Eden Valley Biodynamic Farm
edenvalleybiodynamic.com.au
Dumbleyung, WA

The Grain Family
thegrainfamily.com.au
Moltema, Tas.

Kialla Pure Organic
kiallafoods.com.au
Greenmount, QLD

Miller and Baker
millerandbaker.com.au
Perth, WA

Powlett Hill Flour
powletthill.com.au
Campbelltown, VIC

Rock Paper Flour
rockpaperflour.com.au
Monbulk, VIC

Small World Bakery
smallworldbakery.com.au
Langhorne Creek, SA

Tuerong Farm
tuerongfarm.com.au
Tuerong, VIC

Whispering Pines Organics
whisperingpinesorganics.com.au
Barellan, NSW

Wholegrain Milling Co.
wholegrain.com.au
Gunnedah, NSW

Woodstock Flour
woodstockflour.com.au
Berrigan, NSW/Liliput, VIC

NEW ZEALAND

Capital Millers
capitalmillers.co.nz
Wellington

Milmore Downs
milmoredowns.co.nz
Scargill

UNITED KINGDOM

farmingGeorge
farminggeorge.blogspot.com
Essex

Felin Ganol Watermill
felinganol.co.uk
Wales

Fresh Flour Company
freshflour.co.uk
Devon

Gilchesters Organics
gilchesters.com
Northumberland

Gothelney Farm
gothelneyfarmer.co.uk
Somerset

Green Acres Farm
agricology.co.uk/field/farmer-profiles/mark-lea
Shropshire

Hodmedod's
hodmedods.co.uk
Suffolk

Nottingham Mill Coop
@nottingham_mill_coop
Nottingham

Offley Watermill
tcmg.org.uk/offley-water-mill-staffordshire
Staffordshire

Scotland The Bread
scotlandthebread.org
Fife, Scotland

Shipton Mill
shipton-mill.com
Tetbury

Tuxford Windmill
tuxford-windmill.co.uk
Nottinghamshire

Wildfarmed
wildfarmed.co.uk

Worsbrough Mill
worsbrough-mill.com
Worsbrough

Yorkshire Organic Millers
yorkshireorganicmillers.com
York

SERVEWARE (US)

Miro Made This
miromadethis.com
Phoenix, AZ

Facture Goods
facturegoods.com
Chicago, IL

Thank you

This book is all about my dad's and my (mis)adventures. But it's my mom, Maureen, who deserves the credit for teaching me how to cook and, more importantly, about the joy of cooking for others. I ran every recipe in this book by her to ensure it had her elegant balance of flavors and color. She contributed the Summer Stone Fruit Salad (page 56) and the Dolmas Pie (page 130). And she'd like you to know that even though the Dolmas Pie didn't get a photo because it was, *ahem*, not very photogenic, it is incredibly delicious.

Thank you to my dad, Jeff, for providing me with endless fodder and funny stories for this book, supplying all the obscure facts and numbers, and leaving homemade loaves of bread on my doorstep. My dad is so proud of me that he's already reserved his copy of the book at the library because, in his words, 'Thirty dollars for a book seems a bit steep'.

Thank you to all our farmer partners past and present, who took the risk to grow heritage grains with us. Jana Anderson, Dwight Bond, and Gary John. Particular thanks for the generosity of Sossaman Farms and the Sossaman family.

Thank you to Arizona's local food pioneer Gary Nabhan, for his friendship and kindness, and for setting us down the untrodden path of White Sonora wheat all those years ago. Thank you to Chris Schmidt at Native Seeds/SEARCH, who helped us source our original White Sonora seed.

Thank you to Chris and Marco Bianco, for giving us the space to start our business, and to chef Robbie Tutlewski for showing us the back-of-house ropes and being one of our first customers and supporters.

Thank you to my agent, Michele Crim, whose belief in me made this book more than just a dream.

Thank you to all my home cook recipe testers; your participation was so helpful and energizing.

Thank you to Aleta Lynch, who dutifully tasted every success and failure that ultimately became these recipes.

Thank you to my wonderful and creative siblings, Jimmy, Moriah, Sam and Camille, who I hope will someday come work for the family business so I can boss them around in a more official capacity. Thank you to all my in-laws, who gave recipe feedback, watched my children, and generally cheered me on, especially Lizzy Shell, who made generous use of her brain power and extensive vocabulary to help me say what I was trying to say.

Thank you to our first miller, Benjamin Butler, who endured the bulk of our growing pains and is the hardest worker I have ever known. And thank you to all the people who have worked at Hayden Flour Mills since its start, especially Debbie LaBell – your competence and leadership allowed me to work on this book without the weight of the business on my shoulders.

Thank you to all our customers, for taking a chance on our unusual flours. Without you, none of this would be possible.

Thank you to Meg Van Brunt, our too-good-to-be-true nanny, who brought peace to our home and somehow kept up with my never-ending piles of recipe-testing dishes on top of it all.

Thank you to Jane Willson and Anna Collett at Hardie Grant for turning this book into a beautiful work of art. Thank you to Rachel Carter for smoothing out my words so beautifully.

Thank you to David Alvarado for coming out of early retirement to shoot this book. I don't know of anyone else who could have captured the wild magic of it all so well. Thank you to Jodi Moreno for taking such care to tell a story with each dish photographed. Thank you to Jason Sutherland Hsu for your technical photography skills, and Brendan McCaskey for doing just about everything, as well as keeping me sane during the long shoot days.

Thank you to my local chapter of Les Dames D'Escoffier, who are always a trove of wisdom and support. Particular thanks to Tracy Dempsey, who helped me bring some of the more complicated baked goods in this cookbook from my imagination to the page.

And lastly, to my husband, Brian, who did no specific task for this book and yet did everything and is everything. Thank you for sticking by me when I bite off more than I can chew, both literally and figuratively. I love you.